GETTING PUBLICITY

David Morgan Rees

DAVID & CHARLES
Newton Abbot   London   North Pomfret (Vt)

British Library Cataloguing in Publication Data

Rees, David Morgan
   Getting publicity.
   1. Public relations
   I. Title
   659.2   HM263

   ISBN 0-7153-8525-9

Typeset by Photo-Graphics, Honiton, Devon, England
and printed in Great Britain
by A. Wheaton & Co., Hennock Road, Exeter
for David & Charles (Publishers) Limited
Brunel House Newton Abbot Devon

Published in the United States of America
by David & Charles Inc
North Pomfret Vermont 05053 USA

Preface

Today, as never before, the competition to attract everyone's attention and understanding, as well as their cash, has reached a pitch of incredible intensity. Effective communication with others is now an essential means of survival in these challenging and rapidly changing times, whether you are a businessman or give your time for the benefit of others. Achieving the right recognition and reputation for a range of products or a service to the community by getting the message through is not a matter of luck, but of skill, knowledge and sheer hard work. It is also being absolutely certain of what you need to say in the first place. Whether faced with apathy, ignorance or hostility, there is no longer any alternative to joining in today's communication battle. Indifference, coyness or ignorance of the resources and techniques of publicity will win few friends and influence even fewer people. 'Nothing succeeds like success' is an old saying, but today the big difference is that you have to be *seen* to be successful. Fortunately there have never been more channels of communication and, with the advent and growth of regional TV and local radio, greater accessibility for those with something to say.

This small book is called *Getting Publicity* because the title allows me to cover many of the possible ways of attracting attention, getting people to listen to what you have to say and ensuring that you win their orders or support. Publicity is a convenient 'umbrella' for public relations, advertising, sales promotion, media contact and all the other parts of the communications 'package'. The practical action points suggested here can range from how to identify and sell a good news story to a local newspaper, do a convincing interview on TV or radio, make a lively speech, arrange a worthwhile sponsorship or the visit of a VIP, plan a seminar or open day, get the best out of an exhibition or decide on whether or not to advertise, to making absolutely certain you are presenting your best face at all times. The aim is not to turn you instantly into a fully fledged public relations officer but to provide a basic understanding of the components and techniques of publicity.

This book is aimed at the company employing up to fifty people just as much as the one- or two-man business, whether a manufacturer, a distributor or a retail shop. It is estimated that in the UK there are more than half a million businesses employing thirty people or less. A voluntary organisation can be any group of people who care about others and the quality of life in their community, and are prepared to do something about it. Whether a hobby or an urgent issue it is one of the most delightful features of British life that so many associations, clubs and societies exist to cater for the special interests and concerns of an immensely wide range of individuals.

Inevitably a voluntary organisation at some stage of its useful life must act as a pressure group if it is to change attitudes, attract people to use its facilities or services, as well as being able to win friends and finance. But *Getting Publicity* will not help you to organise bigger and noisier 'demos'. Neither is it a guide to running charities. There are other books specially devoted to these subjects. *Getting Publicity* is aimed at people who make and/or sell a product, provide a service, or who have decided to make some other contribution towards helping their fellow human beings. These two groups of people have a great deal in common because, with limited finance and time at their disposal, each has to make things happen in a lively and interesting way and be resourceful and versatile. But in either case, there is no excuse for not being businesslike. People want satisfying, well-planned, cost-effective action, not just woolly, worthy talk. Inevitably there will be sections in the book which may, at first glance, seem to be directed exclusively either to small businesses or to voluntary organisations, but by cross-fertilisation each type of reader may benefit, finding ideas of common interest and usefulness.

Besides generating more business and greater opportunities for helpful communication between people, I hope one of the best products of this book will be the creation of goodwill. This curiously old-fashioned word, once valued as an asset in a company's balance sheet, is still one of the most valuable assets any individual or organisation can possess. Goodwill towards a business or a body of people, created by an understanding of its aims and activities amongst the many different people who come in contact with it, is the result of successful publicity.

Contents

1
Public Relations and Advertising

People have funny ideas about publicity. They either hate it and shun everything to do with it, or they indulge in it by fits and starts, as a last-minute rescue operation or an ad hoc expedient. They have misconceptions, prejudices and false expectations: if it's *free* then it's public relations; if you have to *pay* for it, it must be advertising. Sadly, the vagueness and sheer ignorance that still hang over the functions and techniques of publicity like a fog waste time and money as well as many valuable opportunities for extra business or support. So we must be absolutely clear what we're talking about—and where the openings and the boundaries lie.

There is nothing very mysterious about publicity, its methods or how they are used. Effective publicity need not cost much money, either. The same principles of good publicity apply whether for a multinational mega-corporation or a one- or two-man enterprise, a sports club or a committee trying to raise money for a piece of hospital equipment.

Advertising and PR

Perhaps because publicity is such a broad term when used to cover a number of promotional or communication activities, it can create confusion. For example, where does advertising fit in with public relations? What is the difference? In reality the function of advertising, by definition, is considerably more limited than is generally supposed, while the scope of public relations is much more wide and deep. The Advertising Association defines advertising as 'any paid-for communication in media intended to inform and/or influence one or more people'. The Institute of Public Relations' definition of PR is 'the deliberate, planned and sustained effort to establish and maintain mutual understanding between an organisation and its public'. Another definition of effective PR is 'good performance publicly acknowledged', which implies the successful creation of goodwill as a result of achievement and progress. Some cynics might say that many have warmed more and more to 'free' PR in a recessionary and increasingly cost-conscious climate because of the lower budgets involved, suggesting that PR is 'Publicity on the cheap'. But that is a misguided view *and* unfair to the growing number of hard-headed businessmen who have invested time, effort and cash in good PR practice for sound business reasons. Pressure groups and others seeking to change opinions and attitudes have come to see that they need to use a much wider armoury of techniques and methods than paid advertising can provide if they are to attract attention.

There are sometimes overlaps between advertising and public relations. Who is to say, for example, whether sponsorship of a sporting or artistic event is strictly one or the other? A paid advertisement in a local newspaper to celebrate a company's fiftieth anniversary can easily be regarded as PR. How *does* PR mesh with advertising? Advertising is a very direct means of stimulating sales by buying advertising space on TV, radio, in newspapers and technical journals, making films, using posters, entering exhibitions, publishing brochures, catalogues and price-lists, producing 'give-aways' and novelties. PR supplements these direct publicity methods. PR itself is never a totally 'free' activity. Albeit at a much lower level of expenditure, it is no substitute for, and should not in any way be in conflict with, advertising. PR can create general knowledge and awareness about an organisation and its operations which support its promotional effort just as advertising can help by more immediate means. Some people argue that you cannot quantify PR results in the same way as you can those of advertising—and that is partially true. Certainly specific techniques can more immediately measure orders or enquiries received against expenditure on advertising space. PR is more concerned with creating understanding and changing opinions, often over a longer period of time. But if simple and clear objectives are set for a PR campaign as for other aspects of running an organisation, there should be no great difficulty in measuring the degree of success. Many a business has been saved by skilful and timely PR—used to break down barriers, clear up misconceptions or reinforce its reputation. No amount of paid advertising can come to the rescue if the goodwill of an organisation is neglected or savaged by other men's opinion.

There are limitations in each case. Advertising costs money but it allows a measure of control over what is said and where and when it is said. In theory you can reach a wide audience. Yet, however much you advertise, you cannot make others necessarily agree with you or buy your products. Indeed, people can be very suspicious of advertising. Public relations works more slowly and through objective appraisal and recognition by third parties. It depends, for example, on the ability of a journalist to interpret or a sub-editor on a newspaper to process the information you give. So you are at the mercy of events. A sudden news story with possibly a more dramatic appeal to a wider audience can crowd your story out at the last moment. Neither is there any guarantee that anything on a specific item will appear at all. Results must be looked for over a much longer time span. Public relations demands patience, persistence and care. A good reputation is slowly earned but quickly lost.

PR is cost-effective

Out of all proportion to the comparatively small budgets employed, public relations can not only be a very cost-effective form of communication but one which creates and maintains the right environment for either a small company or a voluntary organisation. It is the total publicity package into which all the other components, like advertising and sales promotion, fit logically and efficiently.

So, good publicity is good public relations, and vice-versa. It is communicating effectively with the many people who need to know and understand your organisation if it is to achieve its aims and objectives: customers, users, donors and subscribers, employees, trade unions, the bank, suppliers, agents or distributors, the news media and the local community. If you win goodwill, you will establish a good reputation and gain support. If you ignore others whose goodwill is important to you, then you risk false and damaging opinion, opposition and downright obstruction. In simple business terms it makes good sense. Even if a company is well established in the market place, a carefully planned and executed public relations effort can build extra sales at very little extra cost. A particular PR initiative—say a paragraph or two about a product in a trade magazine as a result of your calling an editor on the 'phone, or sending him a press release—can stimulate enquiries for a salesman to follow up.

If starting up a business, an intelligent PR effort will help to gain recognition and acceptance from a host of people whose goodwill and support is vital. If you need help from a supplier, you will find he will be much more willing to give it in times of strain or technical difficulty. Being on good terms with your bank manager, because you have taken the time and trouble to develop the right relationship, is an obvious insurance policy when any financial difficulties arise.

The vulnerability of small business

A small business can be particularly vulnerable as far as its reputation is concerned. Although the chairman or chief executive may attract the glare of publicity, the big companies can take some form of refuge for a time in corporate anonymity, in the sheer safety of numbers. But a small company is very much open to view. People's trust and confidence have to be won and maintained. Yet, because of the power of investigative journalism in the media, there is the very real danger that people can be left with an impression of crafty, fly-by-night businessmen running small shoestring operations, who tend to exploit the customer or simply lack the total experience and skills found in large companies.

Effective public relations makes just as much good sense for a voluntary organisation as a small business. A voluntary organisation needs to create confidence and credibility as much as an awareness of what it seeks to achieve or can offer others. This can be more difficult to accomplish because such a group is dependent on individuals' enthusiasm and the free time they are prepared to give. In the case of a charity, there is a far greater need to succeed for basic humanitarian reasons. But in today's clamour for attention, any charity has to compete as effectively as any commercial venture in its communications effort. The publicity must quickly establish enthusiasm and sympathy for its aims. It must overcome people's natural reluctance to give money for activities which some may feel should be the responsibility of the welfare state. This means making donors believe that their money is not only for a good cause that can realistically be achieved but that donations will be wisely used by an efficient and cost-effective administration.

The art of selling is acknowledged by the professionals to make the customer aware of the unique benefits which a particular product offers. So the art of PR is to make people aware of the special qualities, interest and scope of your own organisation so that they come to know you better and appreciate you more than your competitors.

2
Fundamental Public Relations

How do you make a start in any effective public relations effort? Quite simply by being absolutely sure you really know who and what you are and why you want to take action. If you do not submit your organisation to careful self-examination, you risk failure. Any PR programme demands full knowledge of strengths and weaknesses, the problems to be overcome and the opportunities to be exploited. Organisations, whatever their size, are like individuals in that no two are the same even if they are making the same product for similar markets or providing the same service. An organisation acts and reacts, and has 'character' or 'personality'. Because individuals run it and because no two people think or act alike, they help to create its uniqueness.

Image and identity
'Image' is a word which is much used and often misunderstood. Do not confuse it with 'identity'. Image is the impression which others have of a particular organisation according to what they have personally experienced or heard. Its identity is its uniqueness, its particular range of activities and the whole way of going about things. But does the image bear any relationship or resemblance to the identity—or is there a credibility gap? That must be established sooner rather than later by some form of research, however simple, whether by canvassing opinions among customers or members of the local community, or by questionnaires specially constructed with expert advice.

But is everyone in the organisation absolutely clear why it is to embark on a PR programme? Confusion and disagreement about objectives could make it all an exceedingly pointless and wasteful exercise. Good PR needs an ice-cold clarity of purpose, not a sentimental woolliness or a 'copy-cat' mentality. It has to be *your* need, opportunity or problem to be solved.

Spend plenty of time discussing what needs to be done. Carefully draw up a list of the principal problem areas and potential solutions, and try to place them in order of priority. Are you introducing a new product, service or facility? Are you misunderstood or merely ignored? Do people have only a limited knowledge of your full range of activities and services? Is there growing opposition in your neighbourhood towards your organisation's latest venture? Are supporters of the club playing a less active part in its programme? Does a key individual in the organisation deserve wider recognition for his or her achievement? How can you raise more money for a very worthwhile local cause? Asking basic questions and then putting them on the table in some form of open discussion is an excellent first step in winning the ideas, enthusiasm and commitment of your colleagues.

Select the key features

Once an organisation knows why PR action is necessary, decisions must be taken on what key features are to be selected and put across to the outside world. It is important to be selective. It is no good putting all the 'goodies' into the shop window at once; a rag-bag of jumbled information will certainly result in an adverse reaction. Is your business stronger on personal service or a wider range of specialised stock than your competitors? Have you a group of well-trained, experienced employees who have been with the company for many years? Or are you a bunch of young, lively minds with plenty of ideas on the boil? Does your sports club offer any facilities which are more unusual or more comprehensive than others in the area? Does your organisation possess individuals with special experience or expertise? Is there a special theme capable of being developed and exploited in your next arts festival? Have you managed to identify and satisfy a special need among disabled people in your own area?

Pick the simplest, strongest features and write a short profile of the organisation in not more than fifty words. This is a very salutary exercise because if you can not describe your organisation succinctly, you have not been sufficiently tough in your analysis. Then start to build a framework for action within which you will work, but don't try to pull the wool over anyone's eyes; don't believe you can be something you are not. It only takes a little time for people to see through any false front. There must be complete consistency between your organisation's identity, the public relations programme you design and the image you wish to create and maintain in other people's minds.

Select the publics

The next step is to select the audience or 'publics'. These must be specific, not the world at large. For example, a company, irrespective of size or product, has an effect upon, or is affected by, many more people than it might at first believe. Start with your own employees. Do they share your commitment and enthusiasm? Do they see the connection between their own financial well-being (and that of their families) and the success and prosperity of the company? Such a gap is more understandable in a large company, but it can also exist in a small company because the boss may take it for granted that everyone knows and cares as much as he does. How many employees would like their kids to work for their company if there were a vacancy? Incidentally, a company's employees can often be its publicity agents. The delivery man or service engineer who enthuses genuinely about his firm instead of criticising it is a real tonic. It is surprising, with a real backing from a company's own employees, how the good word gets round in club or pub.

Outside the company, existing and potential customers must be considered. Some may drive a pretty hard bargain on price but it is not always like that. A time will come when a customer will run into a problem which he has not had to face before—and it would be good to think that he will turn to you for help because he has a much clearer idea of the scope and talents of your company rather than just favouring a company offering a keenly bargained price. How much better one responds to a particular firm, not only because their work is good but also because the person who runs it stimulates an interest in the way his firm runs, taking the time and trouble to keep one up to date with some of his new developments which, in effect, enhance his marketing effort. That is a simple example of good business communication.

Suppliers and dealers

And what about suppliers? Whether large or small, their goodwill and support are important to both the small company and the voluntary organisation. With the increasing use of computers, there is the danger of some hiccup and, because of a lack of understanding, a carefully guarded credit rating is lost. It pays to keep suppliers well in sight from a PR point of view, so that an organisation remains credible as well as credit-worthy. Adding their names to the mailing list when you do a mailing shot to your customers or clients might help.

If your company sells through dealers, they are an important 'public' with whom to communicate effectively. You are very dependent on their support and enthusiasm. Inevitably they have to divide effort and time over a number of different lines and there is always the danger that your products can trail behind if you are not vigilant. Making every effort to involve them when there is a suitable opportunity—an interesting order, the visit of a particularly important customer—is good PR and good business. Handled in the right way a dealer can be a very helpful channel of communication with those customers who are otherwise difficult to reach. Even with a limited promotional budget, the small company must bear the dealer well in mind in planning sales literature or advertising, however modest.

Whether a small company or a voluntary organisation, there is a surprisingly large number of other people whose goodwill is important: your MP, the mayor, your local councillor and his permanent officials in the council offices, the local press, neighbours in the immediate area where you have your premises, the police and other local service chiefs, educationalists, chief executives, public relations and personnel officers in local industry and secretaries of other organisations which serve your community. These are the 'opinion formers' or 'opinion leaders' because they can influence the opinions or attitudes of others. Including them is more than an obvious courtesy: failure to do so could risk considerable ill-will.

Getting the 'message' across

The medium is as important as the message. Do you know how your target audience obtains its essential information? Where do you yourself look if you want to be better informed? Do you depend on your local newspaper, trade magazine, TV or your local radio station? Would a series of special presentations, open days or 'teach-ins' be effective, using simple visual aids, or a more elaborate audio-visual programme? Would some form of sponsorship or competition help to create greater awareness of your organisation? Should you use direct mail, leaflets distributed by hand, posters or an insertion in the small ads section of the local newspaper?

Paid advertising is obviously a crucial question. Buying space will depend both on funds and communication needs, but the choice of whether or not to spend money must be made only after it is clear beyond reasonable doubt that the same results could not be gained by a more gradual programme of informed editorial comment in the columns of newspapers, magazines or on TV and radio, by issuing press releases or briefing journalists. A paid advertisement *may* produce enquiries or orders, donations, subscriptions or offers of help, but is the cost justified? How widely scattered is the target public? Local or national? Are the individual members of this public likely to respond better to an advertisement with a clip-out coupon for mailing or to the objective reporting in a publication on the activities of an organisation? Is a one-off response needed or a series of reactions over a longer period? Is the product offered or the service provided really capable of being advertised effectively on a low budget? Would not the cash be better spent on leaflets or in lively media relations? Would it be wiser to wait until more funds are available, when carefully planned advertisements can be used to far greater effect as a balanced component in the next stage of the total publicity programme? Are you certain you are capable of dealing with what could be a flood of enquiries, requests or orders? Even a modest amount of paid advertising (as well as information released to the press for possible editorial coverage) could stimulate a surprising level of response. If you fail to live up to people's expectations and cannot handle correspondence or 'phone calls efficiently, then you could waste your money *and* suffer a serious dent in your reputation.

Campaign of action

Knowing what to say and deciding how best to get it across to a key public lead on directly to the need to design a plan of campaign with a detailed programme of publicity action. The character of the organisation as well as its chosen PR objectives will indicate the necessary style of the campaign, whether a high, aggressive profile needs to be projected or a more sober image created. The PR campaign for a new consumer product or a new leisure facility might demand a much higher PR profile than, say, a charity specialising in helping the victims of rape or assault. In most cases a campaign must have both long- and short-term objectives which can be realistically achieved, some carefully set time limits and then the means of evaluating success at each stage. The vital thing is not to be discouraged by disappointments and to be willing to learn from mistakes.

Objectives and time scales, as well as the degree of emphasis, will be affected by what is being publicised. The launch of a new industrial product would probably concentrate on achieving penetration first of the UK market and then, with proven success and an encouraging cash-flow, would involve a longer-term campaign in selected export markets with the help of the Central Office of Information (COI) Export Publicity Service in circulating information to local media abroad, as well as the use of the BBC Overseas Service. A voluntary group formed to create awareness of a particular local social problem, or to raise cash for a badly needed piece of medical equipment might wish to have a programme of urgent action, whereas a club wishing to expand membership might need much more time to build up interest. A local arts festival might choose to devote an initial effort to ensuring local support and finance before seeking wider audiences and sponsorship.

The penalty of living in the age of mass-media communication is that, because there is so much of it in our daily life, people can only absorb a certain moment of information by eye or ear at any one time. After a while they switch off or put their fingers in their ears. So the challenge is to be imaginative and ingenious in putting a particular story, message or point of view across, to be noticed and listened to. But above all there is always a responsibility to be interesting and informative, helpful and businesslike. To be inaccurate, evasive or downright boring is unforgivable!

3
The Media

'I'm with you on the Free Press. It's the newspapers I can't stand.' Tom Stoppard's line in his play *Night and Day* neatly underlines the innate contradictions of our attitudes towards the media. Few of us could do without some form of newspaper, magazine, radio or TV programme in our daily lives, and yet our regard for editors, producers and journalists is at best ambiguous and at worst hostile. Despite the remarkable choice and quality in this country, our recognition of the total press freedom which we enjoy here is grudging. On an average day, nearly three out of four people in Britain over the age of fifteen read a national morning newspaper and about one in two reads an evening newspaper. Our trade and technical press is highly respected around the world. BBC Radio and TV have won the envy and respect of international media people and general audiences alike, as has commercial TV. BBC and commercial local radio has added another positive dimension to our listening habits. The balance, coverage and sheer professionalism of the British media have given us a window on regional, national and international affairs which other countries, including the United States, find hard to match.

So why are some suspicious of the media? Journalists are often made the scapegoats of industrialists, trade unionists or politicians. Such an attitude can be a convenient 'ploy' by many who seek power and influence and yet try to avoid the attentions of newsmen, but for the rest of us, dislike or suspicion of the media usually arises from ignorance or lack of understanding.

Yet this blend of ignorance and suspicion means that we may miss many worthwhile opportunities as individuals who have something to say to further the objectives of our respective organisation. Sound media relations provide the essential extra arm to our publicity effort. Because the media are so valuable to us and so richly endowed, it is worth taking time to seek the best opportunities to communicate effectively via the printed or spoken word or televised image.

For simplicity, let's divide the media into the printed word and the spoken word, which includes TV. In addition, there are hidden media and a host of other media 'aids' such as posters, direct mail, handbills and other literature delivered to office or home.

The printed word

There are over 120 daily (Monday to Saturday) and Sunday newspapers and about a thousand weekly newspapers. This number includes specialised business, sporting and religious papers and those in foreign languages to cater for minority ethnic groups. The elaborate network of regional and local papers in the UK counterpoints the massive coverage in the 'national' press. An extraordinary sub-media world exists in the 'alternative' press which caters for very specialist interests, community and fringe groups and in the proliferating 'free' papers which are primarily advertising outlets (now over 12 million copies are printed in the UK). There are also over 800 'house' publications produced by industrial companies or public services for their own employees and/or clients.

The 'house magazine' or charity newsheet can, incidentally, be a channel of communication with a very much wider audience than its target readership. If it is bright, interesting and 'newsy' enough and is mailed on a regular basis to selected journalists, it will become regarded by them as a regular source of news items for their own programmes or publications.

The national press

Ten morning daily papers and eight Sunday papers circulate as national newspapers, ranging greatly in editorial weight and style as well as format, from *The Times* and *Financial Times* to the *Daily Mirror* and the *Sun*. Wales has one daily and four evening papers, Scotland six morning, five evening and four Sunday newspapers while Northern Ireland has two morning newspapers, one evening and one Sunday paper.

Each of the national newspapers is a potential outlet for stories of individual enterprise, technological achievement and personal endeavour, though the pressure on space of international and national news means that it must be a story of exceptional quality to catch the editor's eye. Good luck and persistence are also needed. But a short paragraph in, say, the technology page of the *Financial Times* has enormous impact and can produce enquiries from many sources in the UK and overseas. Many of these papers, however, now appear to bend over backwards to feature news of small business achievements as well as interesting community or ecological initiatives. Some papers, for example the *Guardian*, have a small business editor. The business sections of the *Observer* or the *Sunday Times* usually feature several stories each week on the success of small entrepreneurs or innovators. There are also education, community and voluntary service feature sections aplenty. A really interesting story about an achievement or development of a specialist or voluntary organisation which alerts us to previously unknown benefits or dangers, ideas which enhance the quality of life or expand services offered to others, should find no difficulty in being noted in the news columns of the dailies or Sundays. Besides coverage by specialist commentators, many of the women's pages in newspapers show an enthusiastic interest in unusual or creative approaches to solving our social or environmental problems.

Local coverage

Important though the national newspapers are, perhaps the richest ground for exploitation today is the regional newspaper, including the local newspaper, which still manages to maintain a vital hold on its readers. There are over 70 morning or evening local dailies and Sundays, and some 650 newspapers appearing once or twice a week in England. Wales has about 60 weekly papers, Scotland over 130 and Northern Ireland 41. The total circulation of the regional morning and evening papers in England, for example, is estimated at over 7 million with the *Yorkshire Post* and the *Northern Echo* having circulations of over 91,000. Circulation figures for regional evening papers are mostly in the 20,000–90,000 range, although the *Manchester Evening News* and the *Birmingham Evening Mail* manage circulations of over 300,000. Most weekly papers are in the 5,000–30,000 range.

Local newspapers continue to exercise a strong community influence despite the impact of TV and local radio. Whether daily, evening or weekly, the local newspaper fulfils the same valuable function as in the old days of the local gossip circle around the parish pump. The extraordinarily rich collection of information is dipped into and relied on by a wide variety of readers. Some local sports teams publish team details and fixtures knowing that these are more likely to be read than if posted up on club notice-boards. Local newspapers are always extremely relevant to anyone proud of the local community spirit. They are an essential means of communication for local businessmen and those who have a need to kindle local enthusiasm and response.

The periodicals

The periodical press, including the technical press, provides a highly professional service for specialist interests. Exact estimates of totals vary but it is generally reckoned that in the UK nearly 6,000 periodical publications (including local free-sheets) exist which are classified as general, specialised, trade, technical and professional. There are more weighty journals specialising in many different subjects, as well as publications of learned societies, trade unions, the armed services, universities and other educational bodies. The weeklies have the highest circulation with *Radio Times* and *TV Times* magazines leading the field at over 3 million copies each. *Woman's Weekly*, *Woman's Own*, *Woman*, *Weekly News* (mainly for Scottish readers) and *My Weekly* have circulations from 820,000 to 1.4 million. Sporting and leisure interest magazines also have an immensely important and growing readership.

Study of the main media directories—*Benn's Press Directory*, *Brad*, *Pims Media Directory*, *PR Planner* and *Willings Press Guide*—is vital for anyone who is anxious to come to grips with the appropriateness of the periodical press to their special publicity needs. The indexing by both subject matter and title is extremely thorough and the detailed information entered under each publication most useful. In the periodical press there is a considerable number of take-overs and mergers of titles. Sometimes staid traditional titles disappear only to re-emerge with new editorial policies and formats. The competition, though not quite so fierce as in the newspaper world, is keen enough to prevent complacency. However, the best way of knowing what publication suits your publicity needs is to go to your local reference library and have a good browse through these periodicals. You will quickly gauge the editorial policies and methods, the range of information covered and how it is treated, particularly the type of illustrations preferred. Much of the secret of successful dealings with the periodical press in particular is to be well aware of the editorial 'flavour' and range of content, as much as the detail of frequency, whether colour is used and exactly when the publication goes to bed (or gets ready to print) each week or month.

The biggest single factor to remember about the periodical press is that it is bought by people who wish to satisfy a specialist interest. The readership is, therefore, usually much more conscientious in studying each page than the newspaper reader who scans it over breakfast or on a commuter train. The enthusiast will keep the weekly or monthly for careful study over a much longer period. The readership of each copy is numerous, copies passing hands until the tired and tattered magazine finally comes to rest in the doctor's or dentist's waiting-room.

Trade and technical

The UK's trade and technical press is seen by its readers as being highly authoritative. Approximately 700 publications exist in this specialist category. The country's leading trade publisher is IPC Business Press with more than 100 titles. About 80 per cent of trade titles are distributed direct to subscribers by post, the majority having a cover price. But a significant number are distributed on a free, controlled-circulation basis with an increasingly close scrutiny of a reader's eligibility to receive each publication.

A casual glance at a pile of different trade publications might, not arouse great interest in the uninitiated reader. But for many in business, regardless of the size of the individual enterprise, these titles are essential reading if they are to keep in touch with the latest commercial and technical development, personnel movements and news of competitor activity. Many are taken home from the office for careful study in after-office hours.

The spoken word

In recent years, the channels for the spoken word and the visual image have become increasingly elaborate as the BBC and commercial networks have developed throughout the UK. In TV we now have four main channels and who knows what proliferation may result from cable TV?

Local radio began in 1967. Now local BBC radio stations have grown up only to be matched by their commercial counterparts around the country. So, to pick two examples, the City of Sheffield and its immediate area is served by BBC Radio Sheffield and Radio Hallam, Newcastle-upon-Tyne by BBC Radio Newcastle and the commercial Metro Radio. The BBC local radio network is set to expand to a projected total of 38 and independent radio to 65 stations. BBC Radio Wales and Radio Scotland have emerged very strongly in their own right with much local language input. Otherwise regional radio has disappeared with London being the pivot of a national network. Former regional television centres like Manchester or Bristol now provide more specialist programmes such as drama or wildlife.

Local radio has established its authority by degrees. Audiences are small but fairly faithful even if they may tune in for short periods to hear a live 'phone-in on an important local subject, or the news of weather and traffic conditions. There is a close affinity with the local newspaper. The reporting staffs are enthusiastic and quick to respond to an interesting news story or topic. Again, a careful study of programme planning and content will be an invaluable guide to the immensely wide opportunities which exist for publicity. Many of the local programme makers still complain that their opportunities are sadly under-exploited by local business people and others who are usually slow to make the first approach. Whether this is because of apathy, coyness or ignorance is hard to say. But there is tremendous interest and goodwill towards all who bother to make an approach to the news desk in each local radio station. Many local radio chat shows and magazine programmes often have real difficulty in filling their air time. They are genuinely interested in good news and even in product information (particularly if it has an employment aspect) and there is always the outside chance that a good interview or magazine spot might lead to national network repeats.

TV is a more demanding and voracious medium than the other media outlined so far. BBC TV or ITV audiences are much larger than any who listen to radio. Because of the massive audiences who follow the 'soap operas' or sport, it is easy to think that there is massive nationwide standardisation. But the more you study the actual programming on BBC TV and ITV, the more you come to appreciate how decentralised TV has become with a fascinating diversity of regional and local programmes. There are many 'opt-outs' of the network which are tailored to specialised and local interests. BBC TV has eight regional stations in England: at Newcastle, Leeds, Manchester, Norwich, Birmingham, Southampton, Bristol and Plymouth.

The most promising opportunities for gaining coverage in

television exist in the various local news programmes which precede or follow national newscasts and in the great many magazine programmes. But it is important to remember always that a clear distinction exists between TV news and TV current affairs staffs, the former putting out news bulletins and the latter making programmes on specific subjects. Each programme and each producer has preferences and idiosyncracies. The BBC's *Tomorrow's World*, though demanding the highest quality of story material with a strong preference for having the first 'bite' at the story, is guaranteed to stimulate a large number of leads and enquiries. Other programmes with a heavy accent on social problems provide excellent chances for those who can demonstrate that theirs is a genuine and reliable organisation. Approaches from maverick bodies, like some of the more extreme pressure groups, have made TV editorial teams very wary. Gimmick ideas are two-a-penny and though there is sometimes a place for these in some programmes, like *That's Life*, most programme makers are looking for fresh, imaginative and intelligent approaches.

The 'hidden media'

What are described as the 'hidden media' principally consist of news agencies which provide a valuable service to newspapers, radio and TV, supplementing their own newsgathering resources. The three main British news agencies are Reuters, the Press Association and the Exchange Telegraph Company. The British press and broadcasting organisations are also covered by Associated Press and United Press International, both being subsidiaries of US news agencies.

Reuters is the world's largest newsgathering organisation and has existed in London since 1851. It employs well over 500 journalists and correspondents in 70 countries and has links with many national or private news agencies which give access to hundreds of local reporters. Reuters is international in its newsgathering and distribution while the Press Association, founded in 1868, is primarily a news agency for home news but also feeds regional newspapers with the international stories provided by Reuters. The Press Association also has an excellent photographic department offering London and regional newspapers a daily service of pictures. The Exchange Telegraph Company, founded in 1872, concentrates on financial and sporting news. Although these news agencies provide a wide service for news stories, they exercise firm editorial discretion so that there is no certainty that any particular story will be distributed. Increasingly these agencies are providing more and more specialist services aimed at the City, politics and industry.

Other representatives of the 'hidden media' include freelance journalists, who either act as 'stringers' (or local correspondents) for national newspapers, making their living by the lineage of stories accepted, and specialist writers who contribute on a freelance basis to a wide variety of newspapers and periodicals. These are sometimes not too easy to locate. The National Union of Journalists, however, publishes a helpful guide to freelancers.

Finally, no survey of the media's organisation would be complete without reference to the Central Office of Information, financed by central government and based in London, but with a number of regional offices and the BBC Overseas Service (with a sizeable grant from the Foreign Office) at Bush House, London. Both these organisations are of particular importance to actual and potential exporters because they distribute an incredibly rich variety of stories of British achievement and enterprise in science, technology and industry. Linked to government-sponsored overseas trade fairs and missions, both can give superb 'free' publicity service in vital export markets.

This has been a brief, guided trip through the 'media maze'. But the more you explore the detail you will discover that the media world is multi-layered and complex, yet incredibly responsive to the newsworthy story. The vast majority of people who work in the media are thoroughly professional and reliable. But the ways in which they gather and process a vast mass of news material and information, often under immense pressure, need to be understood thoroughly if there is to be a healthy relationship in our increasingly 'open' society today.

The media world is well established and curiously traditional. Yet all branches of the media are now beginning to be challenged by rapidly developing information technology. Optical fibres are, literally, giving telecommunications the speed of light while satellites have turned our world into the 'global village'. Teletext developments, via specially adapted TV sets, like British Telecom's Prestel, the BBC's Ceefax and ITV's Oracle, are already making an important impact on the way news and information are transmitted and received in our daily lives.

4
News Presentation

'Why is there so little *good* news around these days?' That is a frequent question in both our industrial and private lives—and it is usually coupled with a strong criticism of journalists for concentrating on gloomy, sensational or scandalous news items. But there *is* a great deal of good news around today in the world of work and in society in general, which is all too often overlooked. Tracking this down and producing an interesting story can make a significant contribution towards improving understanding between people, stimulating interest and increasing involvement. Publicising solid achievement, say, in the local evening newspaper is an excellent way of both attracting favourable attention and saying 'thank you' to those involved.

Perhaps one of the biggest communication challenges today is to recognise and present good news in an interesting way so that a journalist or TV news editor will take note and 'buy' it. Effective public relations, via 'newsy' information to the press, is a simple and positive way of underlining an organisation's strengths, or explaining its activities and bringing them to the attention of many of the people whose support and goodwill are vital to its success. Usually this can be much more telling than advertising.

What is 'news'?
Can *you* recognise a 'news' story when you see it? News is a mercurial, transitory commodity. 'News is what a chap who doesn't care much about anything wants to read. And it's only news until he's read it. After then it's dead', as one character says bluntly in Evelyn Waugh's novel *Scoop*. We all recognise news about other people. We are led on by teasing or sensational headlines to read about an individual's activities and affairs. If we spent a little time analysing those stories to find what interests or impresses us, we might be more able to recognise what makes a good story and apply the lessons to our own organisations.

Journalists are basically interested in good news or bad news. These are where we are most likely to come into contact with the reporter with pencil poised or microphone at the ready. However, there is a third situation—where you and the journalist meet when there is no sudden drama or startling disclosure, to get to know each other better and to have a 'background briefing'. This can be a valuable form of insurance in moments of trouble and pressure. The better you know each other and the more a journalist understands your organisation and its aims, the less likelihood there is of misinterpreting the facts or writing a story out of true context. It won't work every time, but it will help most of the time.

There is a subtle alchemy which the skilled and talented journalist brings to a news situation. The indifferent journalist will merely record what he or she sees at first glance or after some elementary research. The man or woman with an extra quality will see a new angle or connection so that their story will have an individuality about it. An exclusive story is what most journalists dream of, but the gifted journalist can create his own exclusivity even when it has been given to a host of competitors.

Don't forget that journalists *do* like an 'exclusive' story to try to keep ahead of competitors. But choose your particular journalist and publication carefully. Placing these exclusive stories is a matter of shrewd judgement so that you don't risk upsetting the other journalists who miss out. Ask yourself whether an 'exclusive' will help you to get more coverage than a general approach? A certain journalist may have shown more awareness and interest in your organisation, or a certain publication gone to greater lengths than others to give wider coverage to events or activities which are important to you. An 'exclusive' could acknowledge this special interest or approach.

The media thrive on odd and colourful detail. How often do we find ourselves reading the small paragraphs tucked away at the foot of a column first before turning to the big stories and the leader page? Many of these 'tit-bits' come from the news agencies but editors are only too delighted when they find them on their doorstep. So you don't have to have a story of earth-shattering dimension or significance before you attract editorial attention.

A cynical view of the media is that events—strikes, accidents, mistakes, misunderstandings, protests—happen but news is a product skilfully manufactured from the raw material of such events. Yet this view is useful because it helps to explain so many of the ways in which the media world operates. Everything we read on the page and see on the screen is 'manufactured'. In this sense, newspapers, TV and radio are providing a product made from the raw material of life which we either want or reject. Most are highly aware of our tastes and needs, and cater to these with immense skill.

It is important to recognise that, as with most other products, there is a production sequence. Time, effort and a great deal of money lie between the event and the product we receive. Understanding this may help our relations with the media. In most cases, with the exception of small-staffed weeklies and other specialist publications, many people are involved in the various stages of manufacturing the news product, so there is plenty of opportunity for error, change of emphasis or substantial alteration to take place.

The making of news
How is news made? At the risk of oversimplification, there are basically three stages in the production cycle which overlap to a certain extent. First, there is the newsgathering or the collection of the raw material itself. This is largely dependent on the skill and training of individual reporters. Surprisingly little news is actually presented to a newspaper, radio station or TV by general members of the public. So there is the big opportunity! Most news is gathered by routine enquiry, checking and rechecking of the police and fire services, telephoning local 'top people', attending meetings, reading through minutes, following an instinct or 'hunch'. As much desk work is involved as leg work. There is a great deal of cross-fertilisation: a local radio programme will quickly follow up a story in the local paper; even a national radio programme, like BBC's *Today*, will take up a story that has appeared in the early editions of the national newspapers and give it its own treatment. Although much material comes from news agencies or from other organisations who send press statements and releases, the majority of the latter is discarded because it is badly presented or is simply not newsworthy.

The second stage is the selection of the right raw material from which to make the news product. The editor sets the overall policy and approach and dictates the production schedule; yet, whether on a publication or a news programme on radio or TV, a key individual in the process of selection is the news editor. He or she decides what will make the right news product on the page or on the air. On larger newspapers, 'copy-tasters' may do a preliminary sifting. Other people may make a specialised contribution to the production cycle; for example, in a newspaper, the editors of the features, entertainment, women's and sports pages.

When the basic mix has been settled, then the final production cycle begins. On a newspaper the sub-editors will work on what reporters and other journalists have written. Much of it will be altered or discarded to fit in with other material or the actual make-up of the page. This is where many criticisms voiced by the general public about media methods can arise. While in theory an individual journalist is responsible for his or her own story, a zealous sub-editor can unwittingly create problems because of pressure on space and time. A headline can cause misunderstandings, too, although often it is only meant as an enticing label on the box.

Even at the very last moment before the presses roll or the programme goes out on the air, vital changes can be made. News 'manufacturers' have to be people with nerves of steel and razor-sharp minds. With all the pressures and the sheer number of individuals involved in the total news-production cycle, it is amazing that so few blunders are made.

The best approach to the media

Returning to the best approach for dealing with the media, some events are naturally newsworthy. Hopefully these will be good news events, like the visit of some VIP or a fine or interesting achievement by someone who is part of, or associated with, your organisation. But there can also be conflict, controversy and rumour. News of this kind seems to travel very fast and you will be dealing with the media whether you like it or not. The secret is never to ignore or undervalue such approaches no matter how inconvenient or time-consuming they may be. You never know when you may need to kindle media interest yourself and if you have been unco-operative or inefficient in your dealings with the press, you may have to spend much time repairing the links.

For most of the time it will be up to you and your colleagues to make the most of the running with the media; not in any manipulative or deceitful sense, but on many occasions you will have to create your own news as part of your planned and co-ordinated publicity programme and then go out and 'sell' it.

News ideas

Start by asking yourself and your colleagues, 'Have *we* got a good news story?' Initially, such a question can provoke cynicism or embarrassed silence until someone starts to fling out a few ideas. Such ideas could include:

* Launching a new product or new design or improvement of an old product.
* Examples of how you have helped a customer, through solving a problem.
* An interesting new customer.
* An unusual or interesting end-use for one of your products.
* Helping a customer through a particularly good delivery/after-sales service.
* Publication of new sales/technical literature.
* A new appointment to a position of responsibility or unusual activity in your organisation.
* A major policy change which affects an organisation's objectives and activities.
* Personal achievement by an individual or group of your colleagues, a deadline beaten or outstanding help given in an emergency.
* An 'event' like an open day of an existing establishment, or opening of new or redeveloped premises.
* Participation in exhibition, or display, or special promotion, also membership of an overseas delegation.
* An unusual or interesting visitor and what he or she can say about your organisation in a special 'quote'.
* A new link between an organisation and others with similar interests and activities with consequent exchange visits by personnel and a potential gain in membership through wider joint publicity.
* Anniversaries or other significant dates.
* A 'stunt' or 'happening' which can be created to interest press photographers and TV (provided there is a logical connection with the organisation and it helps to explain an activity or promote a product).
* The 'numbers game', where the umpteenth order is delivered, person helped, member enrolled or donation received.
* A traditional activity reintroduced in a new form or involving a new audience.
* Reviewing a year's activities.
* Announcing the organisation's future plans or detailed programme.
* The sponsoring of a project, particularly if it is the 'first' of its kind.

No news without people

People like to read news with impact on matters which are important, informative and topical as well as diverting or unusual. Virtually no story is news if it does not involve people. Earthquakes and other natural disasters lack that vital, special dimension if there is no reference to the effect on people's lives. What adds to the journalist's enthusiasm and our interest as readers are people's comments or observations in a really good quote. Even details of a person's age and residence appear to add to our satisfaction, providing extra 'colour' to the story. A good photograph, too, with plenty of human interest in it makes an extra contribution, however graphic the journalist's skill with words. A radio or TV story is suddenly given immense lift if there is a colourful series of quotes to balance the reporter's observations or plenty of footage of people involved in or reacting to a news item. News is about what we do as individuals at work or in our leisure lives as we pursue interests, help others, or simply realise some of our dreams.

5
Dealing with the Media

If you have a worthwhile 'good-news' story, what is the simplest way of exploiting it? If it is something you would like to see in the local press, first assemble all the facts, noting them down briefly on paper, in the same way you would prepare for an important telephone call to someone you want to impress. Then ring the news editor of your local newspaper, asking for him or his deputy and making sure you use their full names, and do your 'sales' pitch, putting plenty of enthusiasm into it. Quickly outline the facts, stress the unusual or unique aspects, and be ready to answer some probing questions. The chances are that if *you* are enthusiastic the news editor will become so too. He may well put you on to a reporter to take down the actual details, so be patient. Or he may wish to send a reporter round to see you or those involved, with or without a photographer. Bear in mind that most local newspapers are thinly staffed and work under great pressure so you will have to fit in with their timetable.

Correct timing is vital. The first edition of an evening paper 'goes to bed' at noon, so there is a mad scramble to deal with all kinds of stories in the newspaper's offices from traffic accidents, to cats up trees, to a factory closure or dispute, between the hours of 9.00am to mid-morning. There is considerably more time with a morning newspaper because the newsgathering goes on through the day, gaining momentum in the late afternoon before selection or copy-tasting begins in the editorial department in the early evening. With a weekly newspaper, which usually appears on a Thursday, the vital days for contact are Monday or Tuesday. Miss a day and you may miss the opportunity altogether. Obviously it is in your own interest to think ahead whenever possible and try to give a news editor some notice of the story or the event. Tuesday is a good day, too, for making contact with a national or regional daily. It is a kind of breathing space between reporting the weekend's events and looking ahead to the rest of the week.

When you want to place a news item or story in the trade and technical or special-interest press you will have to produce a press release and send it to the publication, anticipating their deadline. Weekly trade publications usually react quickly in their newsgathering but it is wise always to contact the news editor as early as possible in the week preceding publication week. Monthly publications are much more complex and need to work a long way ahead of their printing and publication dates. Because of these long lead times, there is not quite the same emphasis on up-to-the-minute newsworthiness as compared with the weeklies, or any guarantee that a story will appear at the time that you would like. Often a story may be left over to appear in the next issue. So don't despair, but on the other hand, don't hope to sell every story to all the appropriate publications.

The press release

Writing press releases or background briefing notes for the press demands some skill in making words work for you in a simple and interesting way, but it also requires common sense. The problem is to put down on paper all you want to say clearly and concisely without omitting anything important. Sadly many press releases are far too woolly, jargon-laden, full of clichés and too long. It is well worth trying to make your press release paper look distinctive (but not gimmicky) so that it attracts news editors' attention but also has a clear relationship with the general appearance or house style of your organisation (see Chapter 7). As you build up a reputation for being newsworthy, so the distinctive heading can be a useful, time-saving 'sign-post' for busy editors. The real skill is in writing a first sentence which encapsulates the whole story in a short, punchy way that grabs the editor's attention. It comes with patience and practice, and from a willingness to obtain advice from others with more experience than yourself. If you look at any story in a newspaper you will see how the opening sentence instantly gives a factual summary and yet encourages you to read on. You will also note that most stories are very short and to the point.

Perhaps there is a whole book to be written on the art of the perfect press release but, in the meantime, there is a simple framework for a press release, which, if followed, will tell the editor as much as possible of what he needs to know so that he can judge whether it is of interest to his readers. Of course, he may be encouraged to contact you for more detail; however, you must try crisply to provide answers to the following questions:

WHAT has happened (or is about to happen)?
WHO was involved (or will be involved)?
WHERE?
WHEN?
HOW (all supporting or explanatory information)?
WHY (any policy reasons involved which give extra credibility or interest)?

Always use strong, direct and simple words in short sentences. Avoid long paragraphs. Be specific and informative and don't be afraid to add a useful quote from a key person to add interest and credibility to the story.

Under a simple, brief headline which gives as precise an indication as possible of the subject, the release must be typed, double-spaced, with wide margins, on one side of an A4 sheet of paper headed with the organisation's name. It should always indicate at the finish exactly who originated the story and precisely how the editor or member of his staff may contact you for further information. No press release should be longer than two pages. If more information is relevant put it in a short, separate background note. And don't forget to date your release. Photographs may be important, and are dealt with in a later section. Cover only one topic in a release. It is better to write separate releases than combine a number of topics in one. Try always to concentrate on results, solutions to problems and end products rather than vague general descriptions or conjecture.

The use of embargoes on press releases (for example, 'Not for publication before...') is a touchy subject. Journalists don't like them but will respect them if there is an obvious justification for their use. An obvious example is where a VIP is due to make a speech or perform some ceremony and you need to give the press advance notice of the speech, or where you need to control the timing of the release to gain maximum coverage. But it is risky; things can go wrong, facts can alter. It is preferable when you have a good story to do your planning in such a way that the press can be given the story for immediate release.

Drawing up the media list

As well as preparing a newsworthy press release, it is important to draw up the most effective list of media to which it can be mailed. That is where careful study of an up-to-date media directory, as well as personal knowlege of who in your target public reads what (or listens or watches in the case of radio and

TV) will pay dividends. Each story tends to dictate the media to be used, and it is wise to check the mix of the list each time you issue a release. It is wasteful and counter-productive to do a 'blanket' release on each occasion. One of the editors' main complaints is being deluged with releases which have no relevance whatsoever to their publications. That is why so many pres releases find their way into the waste-paper basket.

A new industrial product for the civil engineering construction industry, for example a mini-computer-controlled attachment for a pneumatic drill to cut noise and save energy dramatically, will obviously be of principal interest to civil engineering/construction journals. But there are many other potential outlets to which a press release on this new attachment, with or without a suitable picture, can be sent. With its environmental and safety benefits, there may be publications which could seize on this product as a means of persuading boards and local government public-works departments to show more consideration for employees and local inhabitants during road, water- and gas-mains repairs. The engineering press will be interested if the component has unusual engineering design and fabrication features. Local press and radio, where the product is made or has been used particularly successfully, could possibly use such a story, as well as a regional 'what's new?' type of TV programme, if the item can be made 'visually' newsworthy. If sufficiently unusual, *Tomorrow's World* might like it. With careful individual treatment the story might make a paragraph in a national newspaper like the *Guardian* or the *Sunday Times* if, for instance, it illustrates a small company's innovative or entrepreneurial drive, or (with a strong 'people' element) a tabloid daily. If the company is prepared to export the product, then the COI or a news agency could be an invaluable additional channel for the story.

A story released by, for example, a local voluntary group which has managed to arrange a special deal for disabled youngsters at their nearest seaside holiday camp would be of prime interest to the local media, not only where the young people come from but also where they will spend their holiday. A 'before and after' story would be of particular interest to the specialist press and also to BBC Radio national magazine programmes like *Woman's Hour* if there are helpful lessons for other groups to be learnt from the experience.

The basic point is to think carefully of your media outlets before you send any release on its way. Often the standard release may need special 'top and tail' adaptation to make it more appealing to a particular publication. It is worth the effort.

Keep a detailed list of the publications mailed for each release (indicating if a captioned photograph accompanied it). This will be a check-list for resulting press clippings and help in future mailing lists. Incidentally, once you have designed your basic media lists, why not have the information sorted and stored on a colleague's or friend's mini-computer with a word-processing facility which can cope with producing self-adhesive address labels? That could save a lot of time and effort.

The feature article

Whether for a newspaper or a specialist magazine, there will be opportunities to stimulate an editor's interest in feature articles about your activities. Again, it is sensible to put down something briefly on paper in the form of a summary of your ideas to send to an editor—and then follow it up with a telephone call. The editor may decide to assign a journalist to write it or, if you are clearly an expert with something interesting and authoritative to say, you may be asked to do the job yourself. Clear jargon-free writing is essential. 700–1,000 words is the average acceptable length. You can always write more later if asked.

Facing up to 'bad' news

These points cover some of the happy news occasions, but any organisation, whatever its size, is bound to have to deal with unhappy occasions or events. All primarily involving or affecting people, these can range from failures, accidents, mistakes and misunderstandings, to technical or safety problems with effluent disposal or noise, industrial disputes, redundancies and closures, a project cut short or financial backing suddenly removed. Unfortunately each of these, while of prime concern to the organisation involved, has a public aspect which cannot be ignored. The debate must on many occasions be carried out in public however much you may wish for privacy. It is very much in your interest to deal with the press as meticulously and efficiently when bad news is involved as when it is good news.

It is very rare for any piece of really bad news to remain private in the business world or the local community. Gossip and rumour flourish. On many occasions when there is a dispute or accident in a company, even employees may decide to 'tip off' the local press. However disloyal this might appear, it is a fact of life and means that when something happens you must be ready for the inevitable call from the press.

It is always much better to meet a tricky situation head on with the press, and not to turn and run. Exercising all the tact and discretion at your command, try to ensure that it is told in words which are as near your own as possible and not via hearsay. 'Refusing to comment to the press will leave journalists and your public audiences to draw their own conclusions, often with disastrous results. Invite the press round and give them the facts which have already been carefully considered. But make sure that all your own colleagues or employees are informed of the news beforehand by you and not via the press.

It is wise to have some simple form of contingency plan which can guide you when in trouble and the representatives of the press appear. You should have clearly laid down rules and procedures for dealing with the press when they make contact. It is important to channel all their enquiries to one point initially, to a person who can deal responsibly with all telephone calls in a helpful and authoritative way, deciding whether or not others should be involved. Failure to make such an arrangement runs the risk of all and sundry talking irresponsibly or inaccurately to any reporter who makes contact. Ideally a senior member of the team should be appointed as public relations officer or spokesman, even as a part-time function. In a small company it is usually best for the boss to do this.

Media guidelines

In dealings with the media, try to follow these guidelines:

1 Never put off a journalist's enquiry with the phrase 'no comment'. Sometimes you may have to be non-committal and cautious, but do it in a friendly manner. If you can, try to explain why you cannot make a statement at that moment and give an indication when you may be able to do so. It helps even more to have a simple non-committal 'quote' ready for the journalist who may be content with half a loaf instead of nothing at all.

2 Try always to answer any enquiry as fully and frankly as you can, without, of course, disclosing anything which may prejudice your story or your organisation. If you don't know the answer, say so and offer to try and find out. Don't make an ill-considered, off-the-cuff statement. You'll regret it!

3 Speed is essential. If an evening paper makes a query at

noon, it is useless to prevaricate or say that the matter will be looked into and an answer provided twenty-four hours later. The information is usually wanted for publication on the same day or not at all. Though delay can sometimes act to your advantage as the story goes off the boil, it is a dangerous 'ploy' to rely on too often. Where incorrect information or half-truths are circulating it is vital to put the record straight quickly. If you have forgotten to say something important or additional facts emerge, 'phone the journalist back as quickly as possible.

4 A helpful and friendly telephone manner is essential. At the same time one must be firm in refusing to be a party to half-truths or sensationalism.

5 Accuracy and reliability are equally important. Keep the information provided to the press as objective as possible.

6 If you are certain that the journalist is trustworthy, you may be able to disclose enough information 'off the record' to enable a story to be written which will satisfy his editor without causing you embarrassment. Remember, it is your own reputation—as well as your colleagues' and the organisation's—you are staking if the journalist proves to be untrustworthy! The 'non-attributable' statement can sometimes be helpful. It is one where you do not wish your name to be disclosed by the journalist.

7 Keeping a promise is vital to good press relations; failure to call back, for example, may be a serious embarrassment. Lack of co-operation will almost certainly guarantee that the wrong story (from your point of view) will be published.

8 Keep a detailed record of all press enquiries and make arrangements to obtain clippings of the stories as they appear in the press. It is a salutary way of learning how journalists use your information and is important for future reference.

Press accuracy
Press accuracy is another touchy subject. Most people have their favourite example of a misprint or mistake. But the press will be more often right than wrong; considering the pressure under which most reporters and sub-editors have to work, it is amazing how accurate they are. A reporter may adapt the details you provide to give the story a slightly different emphasis. It is part of his training to be objective, finding out, where appropriate, both sides of the story, yet his skill lies in making it readable so that it catches the reader's attention and holds it. If there is a serious mistake, call the news editor to ensure that a correction is made

in the next day's paper. But if it is a minor error, don't bother to waste time. Journalists can seldom let an interviewee see what has been written before it goes to press because of the frantic pressure under which most journalists work and, in any case, it is a rather impertinent expectation. But where matters of technical detail, finance or complicated statistics are involved, the wise journalist will be happy to let you check the facts if there is time, but not vet his style, comment or opinion!

The press conference

Calling a press conference is an important step to take. Often this is preferable to a series of involved telephone calls and ultimately may save time and effort all round. It is a businesslike way of drawing together a number of loose threads. Unfortunately, you may not have all the journalists you wish to talk to at the conference, so you will end up still having to telephone some of them. On balance, it is better to deal with significant or difficult news by talking face to face with a group of reporters or individually. You have an instant means of seeing whether or not they have understood your message and you give them a better opportunity to clarify points through questions. Some experienced people in public relations who have many long-standing close contacts with journalists, find that a quick chat on the telephone is sufficient because great trust and understanding exist between them. But that will not necessarily work for beginners who have to learn how to build such a relationship through personal contact.

The golden rule if you are inviting the press round on your initiative is to be sure that you *do* have a good story to tell. Ask yourself whether calling a press conference is really necessary? Journalists hate wasting their time and editors hate it even more. If you study the story carefully, you may find that it can be adequately told in a press release. On the other hand, if the story is strong with plenty of interesting detail, if there is something to see as well as a good opportunity for journalists to meet a number of people involved in its development, a press conference should produce better coverage. But try always to give plenty of notice when you issue your invitations, particularly if it is a non-urgent, non-sensational type of story. Always avoid the end of a week—or a Monday when there is a lot of catching up to do in editorial offices. Tuesday or Wednesday is a good bet for most publications.

You may find you have to spend much time 'phoning round to check if journalists have received the invitation, can come or need to be reminded to come! Journalists have many demands on their time. You must make sure you and any colleagues involved take and keep the initiative. If you don't, you are risking a great deal because most journalists are shrewd people and will run rings round you if they deduce you are vulnerable, evasive and badly organised. So the emphasis is on being prepared. The whole occasion must be planned carefully and for such an important situation you must make time. The planning must extend to trying to anticipate the journalists' questions and preparing your answers. The meeting must be structured and always try to do a rehearsal of special presentations, checking for running time and the correct functioning of any visual aids. You must decide who will be in the chair to control events. You must organise a simple timetable to allow time for presenting the story, dealing with questions and carrying out any necessary visit or tour. A statement must be prepared with sufficient copies run off in advance for the numbers attending and handed to reporters on arrival after you have introduced them to the other attending members of your organisation. They should be given a chance to read through this and then ask what questions they like. Be hospitable; provide simple refreshments: coffee or tea and biscuits will usually suffice, unless it is close to a meal time. This helps to break the ice and give the reporters an opportunity to get to know you. Don't forget that you can win a lot of goodwill among journalists if you can add some little element of surprise to a press conference: an unexpected chance of being able to meet interesting employees, customers or clients or a quick tour of your organisation. Even a very small, inexpensive give-away (perhaps even something you make?) can arouse interest. *But* don't risk these details being a distraction from the main point of the press conference. If you're in doubt, don't! The best advice is always to consider how you can make sure your press conference is efficiently run, worthwhile for the journalists attending and, if appropriate to the event, enjoyable. Make sure you know exactly who attended. Use a visitors' book and try to persuade them to sign in clearly, including the name of the publication.

Where detailed aspects are involved, it is always best for those who have a close knowledge of the situation to be present to handle these. It helps to add interest as well as credibility.

Sometimes journalists can be suspicious if one dominant personality does all the talking while colleagues refuse to be drawn.
But it must be decided in advance what issues cannot be tackled
in the conference or where it may be necessary to give a certain
amount of information 'off the record' to explain something that
the reporters obviously find puzzling. Remember that if this *is*
the case, any remarks must be prefaced by the fact that this is off
the record and not for quoting. Be prepared to let reporters use
your telephone if they are up against a deadline.

Because most local evening papers appear in the early or
mid-afternoon, try to call the press conferences for not later than
11.00am. This will give the reporter time to write his story for the
first edition. But specially urgent considerations may, of course,
warrant a later time, provided the reasons for this are made
clear. A mid-morning conference will suit most journalists on
morning papers or specialist publications, though travelling
distances and transport arrangements must be considered.

A press seminar or 'teach-in'

On occasions, it is very effective to hold a press seminar or
'teach-in' on a more elaborate basis where you have a story
which is packed with interesting and important detail and it
warrants treatment in depth. This is useful where you have a
technical development to promote involving several contribu-
tors, or you may wish to invite a careful consideration of a major
problem which your organisation is tackling. But be very sure of
your ground before you set it up, otherwise it could be a most
damaging 'non-event'. Allow plenty of time to plan the event in
every aspect. It is best to have a small project team to determine
the salient points of the story, prepare short presentations with
or without appropriate slides or diagrams on flip-charts and
organise the actual programme. A typical programme might be:

10.45am	Assemble: coffee.
11.00am	Introduction (objective of meeting and details of prog-ramme).
11.10am	First presentation.
11.30am	Questions and answers.
11.45am	Second presentation.
12.05pm	Questions and answers.
12.20pm	Tour of plant or premises with carefully briefed guides.
12.45pm	Buffet lunch.
1.30pm	Disperse.

It will usually be necessary to provide some back-up material for such an event which includes the principal points you are trying to get across and any helpful background information, including a list of names and functions of you and your colleagues. Though most journalists will write about what they find interesting or relevant to their readers, they will appreciate such background information in crisp summary form to refer to when they are back at their typewriters, particularly if there are significant facts and statistics which need to be included.

TV or local radio

So far we have concentrated on dealing with the newspapers or the trade press, but you must never overlook the possibility of approaches to or from either TV or local radio. Or there may be an incident or event involving you or one of your colleagues where the local TV or radio station seeks you out for an interview which you would much rather avoid. Again, you must ask yourself whether it is in your best interests to do so. Would it not be wiser in the circumstances to face up to things and put across your point of view, your explanation or clarification?

'Surviving' the interview

It is not possible to go into the considerable amount of detail here that is necessary to cover fully the preparation necessary for 'surviving' TV or radio interviews. There are a number of books on the subject which give a good grounding. There is also an increasing number of specialist trainers who give excellent practical advice and tuition in a studio environment. Some trainers address groups of people which can cut the cost, and sometimes there are opportunities for free tuition under the wing of a sponsoring organisation.

Each interview on TV or radio is an invaluable opportunity for you to promote your point of view, good news story, policies' or product—on your terms and positively if you go into it with your eyes open. It is obvious that trade unionists and politicians, whatever they may say about the press and the media, are taking the fullest advantage of these opportunities far more effectively than many of us. But the few representatives from business or other institutions who know their way around the TV and radio world, score heavily in interviews, giving as good as they get from sharp interviewers.

What skills are necessary? Not many—and these are simple.

Chiefly they consist in being able to put your facts or point of view across concisely and with credibility. Take a lively interest in the technology of TV and radio and the techniques of interviews. You will never overcome that flutter in the stomach and the dry mouth before you go on the air or appear in the TV studio, but ignorance isn't bliss. Neither is over-confidence, whether it arises from belligerence through wanting to take a rise out of the interviewer, or from alcohol taken to give you Dutch courage. So it is vital to stay cool and collected even if you can't be calm.

Each interviewer, as a result of training and experience, can quickly weigh you up and evaluate your story. You must watch his or her skill by deciding what the three or four most important points are that you want to convey. Usually you will have only about three minutes in which to speak. When you are asked to do an interview, find out what is expected of you—the line or format of the programme, whether it will be live or recorded—and then get all your ideas together. Don't expect to be given all the likely questions in advance. Select that vital trio of points, putting them in order of priority. Then decide when you are asked the leading question that you will get a chosen point across as the first part of your answer, rather as one tries to get the nub of the story in the first sentence of a press release. Having made it, you can then strengthen it with interesting supporting facts or figures. Even if you have only managed to register one of your priority points with conviction, you will have made a significant impression which will benefit you and your organisation.

Always use simple words and short sentences. Be direct; don't prevaricate. If an interviewer asks slanted questions or makes a statement that is patently wrong, politely but firmly correct him by spelling out the correct information as concisely as possible. If you stand your ground properly, others watching or listening will respect you as an expert on your subject. If an interviewer should try to be snide or make fun of you or your organisation, don't get rattled. Resist the temptation to descend to the same level. Instead just make sure you get your own key point across before it is too late, perhaps saying, 'OK but do you realise that it is...', adding some important statistic or example. Your one sentence, firmly said, can be very telling.

Pay very close attention to what the TV floor or radio studio managers tell you so that you know what signs to observe and what is expected of you in front of camera or mike. A little self-awareness is important. Mostly we are unaware of our personal mannerisms or habits of speech. The over-use of cliché and jargon or a verbal tic—'you know' prefacing each sentence or cliché phrases like 'at this moment in time' instead of 'now'—are as irritating and distracting as the coin-jangling, unguarded nose-picking or scratching. Always be sure to sit up properly in your studio chair. Never slouch. You will be a much more positive and effective individual during an interview. Building up your personal strengths as a communicator under pressure, being aware of and minimising your weaknesses will give you self-confidence. When you are on 'the box', why not get a colleague or friend to record you on a video cassette? On play back you could learn how your technique could be improved.

A final point: keep an up-to-date directory of the contacts you build up from newspapers, TV and in radio (and all other valuable contacts for that matter) with their telephone numbers. This is particularly important when you have met journalists with a specialist interest or who have proved to have a sympathetic interest in your activity. Try to develop a positive working relationship with publications which are important to you. If you can spare the time to visit your local newspaper or leading specialist publication, besides forming valuable personal contacts, you may learn of some useful story 'gaps' from an editor, feature writer or reporter, which your organisation may be able to fill. Keep an eye open for opportunities to visit your local TV or radio station. Occasionally they have 'open-house' events for interested organisations to learn more of what goes on and what material is needed for broadcasting.
You will meet many interesting and informed media people. By dealing with them intelligently and taking a close interest in what they write or say, you come to learn what makes good news and how you can use this to your advantage. They in turn will value you as a sound and interesting source of information. Journalists can become infected with enthusiasm for causes like anyone else. The small businessman or voluntary worker who can genuinely interest a journalist in what he or she is trying to do can have a valuable ally. But never forget that journalists' professional loyalty is always to their publication, TV or radio programme and, however friendly the working relationship, don't for a moment imagine that you can have them 'in your pocket'. That would be an insult to their integrity—and yours.

6
Photography and Audio-Visual Aids

Getting good publicity photographs is not easy. Indeed, it can be surprisingly difficult to make people understand that, whether for general or specialist PR purposes, publicity photography is something that demands great care in arranging and high quality in the finished results. Yet good photographs are an immensely strong and effective publicity aid in print and also add dimension and interest to a TV studio interview if video or film coverage is not available.

It is well worth while studying the whole subject in detail to discuss and decide what is right for your own promotional effort. It is important to look at other people's promotional material and examine their photography. You will quickly come to recognise what type of photograph works well for their purposes but, sadly, it may not be as easy to be similarly objective when examining any of your own efforts.

The first fact you must face is that good photography costs money, unless you are lucky enough to have enlisted the direct help of a top-flight photographer who has agreed to support your activities at little or no cost in return for including your work in his portfolio for exhibition. Sadly, there are a great number of very average professional photographers who treat your needs as a routine rather than a special assignment. Also, there are trendy photographers who, conditioned by work for advertising agencies, insist in charging high fees in the belief that at that price the client will think the work must be good. There are also many photographers who are convinced in their minds that they know much better than the client what is wanted. They will listen to your brief with either a sad, tolerant smile or signs of growing impatience—and then go away and do precisely what they, and not the client, want. However, the photographer may have years of experience and be able to contribute useful ideas.

The second problem can arise from the well-meaning efforts of colleagues who, equipped with sophisticated photographic equipment believe they can produce just the photograph you need to aid your publicity effort. Equally a set of marvellous pictures may arrive on your desk unannounced; you then find out that they are of some event that happened six months ago and your colleague did not send them to you before because he was waiting to finish the film in his camera! It requires a mixture of tact and firmness whether you are dealing with a friend or your helpful colleague—you are very dependent on their goodwill as a source of vital information which may lead to excellent stories. One must be frank and explain why the offerings are not suitable—and yet also contrive to offer encouragement.

Thirdly, there is the fact that competition for space for photographs in the industrial pages of newspapers and in technical magazines is keener than ever due to rising print costs. The vagaries of advertising support in an uncertain economic climate must make picture editors' jobs extremely difficult. In many cases, too, journal editors are only interested in work which they commission themselves.

Every picture tells a story

What is the purpose of a good PR photograph? That must be asked each time you embark on a PR exercise whether to sell a product or promote an activity. Remember the old adage that 'a good photograph is worth several hundred words of 'copy'? People tend to be attracted primarily by visual images. This is particularly the case today when audiences have become conditioned by television and colour supplements and seem no longer to have the ability or wish to concentrate on words alone. So a good photograph must be able to grab your chosen target's immediate attention and interest. Since nowadays the chances of having a sequence of photographs printed in the shrinking pages of journals is slight, each picture must as far as possible try to tell a complete story. It must be the cake upon which the caption or the accompanying paragraph is the icing. It must be a focal point for your news story or add the right extra dimension to your promotional literature. It can be the visual key which unlocks the story you have to tell by pinpointing a message, a technical detail, event or achievement.

Bad PR photography can be immensely damaging to your cause. It denotes amateurism and a slipshod, even unreliable, approach to running your affairs. Instead of encouraging people to read the accompanying words, a bad photograph can distract their attention and form a distinct communication barrier. But good photographs will be a stimulus and a support in your PR effort, so what practical steps can you take to ensure better photography?

'Free rides'?
Firstly, you can rely on others' efforts in a variety of ways. For example, where a straightforward publicity effort involves people, thereby focusing primarily on the human interest, you can aproach the news or picture editor of your local newspaper with the idea of a picture news story. The more exciting a visual image you can paint in their minds, the more likely they are to send a photographer. Or you can co-operate with others who have more money than you to spend on a photographic assignment. Perhaps you can seek the involvement of a local company's employees in your affairs so there is a possibility that the PRO will tackle the story for his own outlets in, say, the trade press or his house journal, letting you have copies of the photographs for your own use. Most PR people are very helpful in this way. It takes time to set up such a deal but it would result in great savings plus additional coverage for the story.

Where specialist or technical photographs are involved, this 'free' photography is not so easy to arrange. But if you are a sub-contractor for a prestigious contract, you may be able to 'hitch a ride' on the photography being commissioned either by the main contractor or the ultimate customer. Increasingly, large companies are anxious to help the voluntary organisation in many practical ways, quite apart from their financial support. Their publicity departments can be very approachable. It is important to take every opportunity to enquire what photography is being carried out so that you can try to join in at minimal cost. There are also occasions when you can benefit from photography which has already been taken for another purpose, say a company's annual report which depicts a project in which you have been involved at some stage. Provided due acknowledgement is given, you may be able to obtain copies of these photographs for reproduction in your own printed material or for exhibition purposes at very little cost.

If such 'free rides' are impossible or even inappropriate, you will have to rely on your own or a friend's efforts or commission a professional photographer. If the former, first seek the advice of others experienced in publicity photography who can be objective about your own or others' efforts. Such advice may steer you towards a more gifted amateur photographer than yourself who may be persuaded to help you on a cost-plus basis. It may be possible that photography students at your local college of art, with the principal's goodwill, could become involved in recording your activities as part of their field work. Such an association could be of mutual benefit. Needless to say, you must be very sure of your ground before seeking this involvement.

Using a professional

If you decide to use a professional photographer, there are a number of practical steps you should follow for the best results. Firstly, and this is obvious, know what *you* as the client want to do in some detail, extending to the point where you should try to visualise the journals or other outlets in which you want the photograph to appear. Many photographers are specialists: you don't want a fashion-biased photographer to take pictures of a factory. Never be afraid to seek advice from others, particularly PROs in lively local companies who will be happy to point you in the right direction.

Having tracked down the right photographer, be prepared to spend time in briefing him thoroughly. Tell him what you want to achieve, how and where you would like the photographs to appear—a magazine, your own printed material, a particular exhibition, etc. Ask him to guide you about whether colour is a justified extra expense. Good black and white photographs can sometimes be more effective and versatile than colour. Yet it may be that the subject actually cries out for colour. Time spent in sorting out the basic approach at this early stage will save costs later and give you an idea of total costs before you are finally committed.

Watch the details

There are a number of detailed points which you should watch:
1 Pictures without people are usually uninteresting unless it is a highly technical and detailed shot. Babies, pretty girls and animals always seem to attract attention. Certainly a photograph will benefit from capturing some form of action in it. When taking photographs of a production sequence in a factory, or a piece of plant which uses your product, it is important to include the operator. This gives 'life' in every sense to the photograph as well as indicating the size and scale of the operation.

2   The irrelevant 'girlie' picture can, in these days of anti-sexploitation, become counter-productive, offending and alienating half your audience—the women. When photographing functions, avoid shots of people guzzling food or drink. Also avoid the 'way out' shot using a fish-eye lens which, in the hands of an average photographer, can be most irritating. A well-composed, simple shot is usually far more effective.

3   If arranging for a set or series of photographs to be taken, try to get the full sequence of the activity involved. Close-ups as well as long shots will help explain what is happening and provide a useful choice for editors or designers to work from. Again, if possible, include the person or, if it is a detail, the person's arm or hand working the equipment. Always ensure that the surroundings are as tidy as possible; litter or clutter in a photograph can be very distracting. Similarly grubby, stained overalls can spoil a shot of people at work.

4   The fuller the information you send with the photograph, the easier it is for more interesting captions or copy to be written. If the operation is part of something bigger, if the product is being used on a special contract, or if the event is part of a programme, background details of these are essential.

5   Be careful to check about any restrictions or acknowledgement which should be observed and who should approve final use of the material.

6   Before going to the expense of ordering a number of full-sized prints, always insist that the photographer sends you a set of contact sheets. If you don't, you may never see the photograph that's exactly right for your job because you are relying on the photographer's judgement. When you have chosen, ask him to mask the photograph when enlarging it in the way *you* want, not his, to help underline the story.

7   Good black and white photographs can often be better than colour photographs, particularly where lighting, climatic or operating conditions are tricky.

8   When supplying black and white photographs to publications, 8½in × 6½in glossy prints are the most suitable. Be sure to mail them flat in a stiffened envelope which should be marked 'Photographs—please do not bend'.

9   When using colour film, you must choose between slides and colour prints. Make sure if using slides that the film can be quickly processed. Ektachrome, for example, can now be processed almost while you wait by a good local processor, while

Kodachrome takes time because it has to be sent to Kodak. Today if colour and black and white photographs are needed, it is probably best to shoot both but at a pinch you can usually get adequate black and white prints off colour negative film. While television and most printers prefer to work from transparencies, new techniques mean that colour prints *can* be acceptable. It is wise to check this with each publication in advance.

10 Before issue to the press, each photograph must be captioned carefully on a separate sheet which should be fixed by clear adhesive (never with staples or paperclips) to the bottom of the reverse of the picture in such a way that it may be read from the front with the picture in view, and folded away. The caption should be given a title which should be the same as on the accompanying press release. It is difficult to write crisp captions but try to describe briefly in simple terms what is happening in the picture, being scrupulously careful to spell people's names (use first name rather than initials) correctly with their designation or title in the order, from left to right, of appearance in the photograph. Add your name and telephone number in case of further enquiries being necessary. Never write anything on the back of the photograph with a ballpoint pen or hard pencil. The pressure will leave tell-tale indentations. Use a very soft pencil if you need to write anything.

11 Keep a note of which photographs, by their negative number and date, were issued to which publications.

12 To save money, try to anticipate how many copies of each photograph you will need before you place the order with the photographer or processing house so you can get the benefit of any quantity discount for prints. It is particularly important, if colour prints are involved, to choose 'economy' or machine-made prints in standard sizes. If you are up against a tough budget and cannot afford a liberal mailing of photographs to the press, concentrate on the priority publications and then indicate that 'photographs are available on request' to the others when you send them your press release. Another idea worth exploring with a processing house is the possibility of a simple promotional aid by using the colour photo-leaflet, which can be quite economical for small quantities.

The audio-visual approach

The repertoire of visual aids is now so wide that it is wise to consider all your options in any publicity effort where pictures are important to you. Audio-visual sequences involving the projection of 35mm colour slides, which can be changed either manually or automatically via a series of pulses on an audio cassette, can add considerable impact in any presentation. Unless you are lucky enough to have an enthusiastic, talented or knowledgeable colleague with all the appropriate equipment, you will have to spend a considerable sum of money with a professional company in making an audio-visual sequence using two projectors with sophisticated cross-fade in and out facilities, commentary and music, even before you buy or hire the equipment for subsequent presentations.

You may, therefore, have to be content with using just one projector and presenting the accompanying commentary 'live' on each occasion. Curiously, audiences will accept the simple, no-nonsense approach but will react badly against the poorly executed, pretentious and over-complex treatment. So, if time and money are really short, opt for the simplest method. Spend what money is available on getting the best 35mm colour slides to illustrate your theme and where you need diagrams make sure that the original artwork is of the highest standard before it is photographed on to slides. In slides of diagrams or charts, many people make the big mistake of trying to cram so much in that it is impossible to read or comprehend even when projected on to a large screen. Keep it short and very simple; thirty words per slide should be the maximum.

Video or movie?
The growth of home video offers tempting prospects as a further publicity tool. But remember that people have become very discriminating, even blasé, in their reactions to what appears on the box. They may put up with the video equivalent of home movies with casual amateurish shots of family and friends on holiday, but they can become highly critical when anyone tries to put a message into another context; for example, when you are trying to 'sell' an idea as part of any campaign or product in a promotional effort.

Unless there is a compelling reason to use video and you have the money to spend to take professional advice and commission a properly made video programme which satisfies your exact needs, it would be wisest to resist the blandishments of this medium until you are very sure of yourself and your whole promotional effort. It *is* very demanding and time-consuming.

Exceptions to this common-sense rule will certainly occur: for example, there may be some unique event taking place which needs to be recorded for posterity when you may not be able to rely on the TV news cameras being present. Though it is becoming easier and cheaper to have video tapes edited professionally by local specialist companies which will remove the weakest parts of your material before you offer it for viewing by your audience, 16mm movie film is cheaper to edit and preferable when large audiences are to be invited. You can make good video cassettes from film but not vice-versa.

Once again, before embarking on a video or film venture, seek advice from others and ask yourself whether a more simple approach would not help to prove your point more effectively. Merely using complex techniques for their own sake will not win you any extra points and you risk everything by trying to be too clever. In the meantime, however, try to take a lively interest in video and film techniques and their potential as important promotional media.

7
Image and Appearance

Have you taken a good look recently at the visual appearance of your own organisation? That means the surprisingly numerous ways in which you present your activities to the various people with whom you come in contact: customers, suppliers, employees, local officials, your bank manager. These ways of presentation include such important visual aspects of a company in action as letterheads, quotation forms, invoices, statements, labels, delivery notes, sales literature and instruction manuals. Then there is the packaging of your product, your van or lorry which delivers it and the premises where the product is made or sold. A good appearance is a vital commercial consideration for a company, but it has just as much relevance for the identity of a voluntary organisation.

Making a good impression with a clean, well-designed appearance is important today. It is as important for the small organisation as for the large. Yet it is no use applying a cosmetic 'lick of paint' if everything beneath and behind is wrong. The superbly designed piece of notepaper may impress initially, but if the organisation is sloppy and slow to respond or the product is badly designed and poorly made, the delivery unreliable and the after-sales service non-existent (or the letter, on the posh notepaper, is badly typed or ungrammatical) people will soon spot the inconsistency.

Usually the best design looks the simplest: that applies as much to a piece of furniture as to an engineering component. But good design does not happen by chance. It results from a keen awareness of its importance. Good industrial design is that which is imaginative, well planned and functional, responsive to users and their environment, and appropriate to and in sympathy with the identity or character of the company. Good industrial design can be capable of adapting to changing tastes and markets as well as technology. It develops as the company develops.

Getting the basics right

Of course it is important to spend time worrying about the basics of the business—the design and performance of the product, the delivery service and the after-sales service, the finances—and getting these right before doing something about the graphics or the visual elements. Indeed many small firms, as a result of increased foreign competition, are now much more aware of the importance of good product design than ever before. They are often closer to their market place than the larger firms and it is easier for the technical, production and marketing people to talk the same language. But it is vital not to neglect how you look to others. A tatty letterhead (or any other piece of printed material from the firm for that matter) makes a most undesirable impression. So, ironically, you may have a first-rate product designed to all the highest specifications and manufactured to rigorous quality controls and yet your customers may think that you are old fashioned or slip-shod because you look that way. People are increasingly interested, perhaps because of the influence of television, in the visual quality of things.

Beware of gimmicky industrial design, particularly when it comes to graphics and printed material. People can be taken for a ride by a slick advertising agency or by inferior design 'artists'. They may think they are getting a bargain by someone offering to produce a jazzy looking letterhead for a modest fee. But it can end up being a liability. Remember that whatever design you buy must be something you and your organisation can live with for some time. It is not a case of trying to be an overnight sensation. Good design is always capable of being adapted as organisations and circumstances alter.

Choosing a designer

Choosing the right industrial designer is not easy. The Design Council, which has centres in Glasgow, Belfast, Manchester, Wolverhampton and Cardiff as well as London, can give considerable help whether through its Designer Selection Service or the Design Advisory Service, a funded consultancy service operated by the council on behalf of the Department of Industry. To establish the exact contribution which the designer can make to a small team, an extract from the Design Council's report published in 1977, *Industrial Design Education in the United Kingdom*, may help:

The precise role of the industrial designer in the development team will vary from one project to another and will depend on the skills and experience of other members of the team as well as those he himself has to offer. In all cases, however, he is likely to be involved to a greater or lesser extent in the following activities:

(a) Agreeing his brief with the client or employer, defining the extent of his involvement in the project.

(b) Establishing the objectives and development stages of the project.

(c) Defining particular product requirements such as production quantities, production methods and costs, target selling price and methods of marketing and distribution.

(d) Investigating the requirements of the product from the user's point of view, such as who will use it, why, where, how and when.

(e) Collecting and analysing information from existing surveys, standards, patents, safety requirements and protective legislation, etc., and obtaining more information where required.

(f) Preparing ideas for the product in sketch or model form, with particular emphasis on visual, social, aesthetic and ergonomic requirements, and collaborating with other members of the development team in making proposals encompassing the mechanical and electrical requirements of the product as well as establishing with the client or employer any innovative features to be incorporated.

(g) Producing or supervising specifications for the design in the form of working drawings, models, prototypes, etc., within such commercial restraints as completion dates, and performance and cost requirements.

(h) Liaising with those concerned with the production stage of the project.

SIAD (Society of Industrial Artists and Designers) publishes helpful guidelines on working with a designer and approximately what fee scales are involved.

Preparing the brief

Preparing the initial brief is a vital part of any design exercise. Be very precise as to why you are taking action; it will save time and effort later. For example, in tackling house style, collect together as many examples as possible of the ways in which your company looks today: stationery, packaging, photographs of your signs and delivery vehicles. The designer will get a much better overall impression of the problems to be tackled and will probably be able to suggest practical ways in which to introduce economies through simplification and standardisation. Don't try to change everything all at once: that would be both costly and wasteful if you hold plentiful stocks of printed material. Draw up as complete a list as possible of all the elements needing attention and put them in order of priority. Stationery will be an obvious starting point for making an immediate impact, but don't delay too long in ensuring that the whole programme can be completed in a time that is reasonable and in line with your budget.

The cost of good design can seem daunting at first glance, but money spent at the right time on product design and on creating a good appearance for your company should be regarded in the same light as investment in a piece of productive machinery. It is advisable to take a good look at the way in which other companies either cultivate or neglect their appearance. You will find that those companies which look good usually perform well and, furthermore, take pains with the detail of their appearance; it is consistent and integrated. Slovenliness is allied in others' minds to carelessness and poor attention to detail and, ultimately, poor performance.

First impressions
It is difficult to over-emphasise the importance of making a good first impression on people when they make contact with you either on the 'phone or when they come to your office or factory. The telephonist and/or receptionist is a vital ambassador for any organisation. They reinforce or dissipate all the goodwill which you and your colleagues have built up. How often do bosses listen carefully to the ways in which calls into their own company are handled by their staff?

This is, in fact, one of the easiest faults to put right. For the untrained there are simple but effective training courses run by British Telecom and other companies. But it should not stop there. Make sure that your telephonist is one of the best informed people in the whole organisation. Take time to tell her (or him) about some of the latest developments—and check that she really understands who does what on your staff. That can save invaluable time and patience for all who contact you. She is a VIP and make her feel as such. If she is the right sort of girl she will respond magnificently. If she isn't, transfer her to another job where she cannot do any harm. An interested girl will develop with training and experience a really warm and positive telephone personality, which can be a great asset.

Reception areas, whether in office or factory, need care and attention. Many people have to spend a lot of time waiting there. So try to make it as pleasant as possible for them and they will be grateful. Visitors are a captive audience so ensure that you have a bright interesting display about your activities, plus a few copies of a simple leaflet about the organisation or products. Perhaps a magazine has printed a short article about your recent achievements: obtaining reprints of this is a cheap way of providing a simple hand-out. The reception area in the works or factory is as important as the office waiting-room. It need not be the hole that so any of them are. Having someone there with a pleasant personality can make all the difference, too. And if you have drink-vending machines in the factory, why not consider locating one in this area?

8
The Case Study as Effective PR

The need for promotional literature about the products or services which your organisation is able to offer might seem a trifle ambitious when margins may be squeezed and budgets modest. But a simple, inexpensive and quick idea is the use of the case study, rather than a glossy brochure produced on the cheap. Concisely written with or without any illustration and printed on one or both sides of a single A4 sheet of paper, case studies about successful applications for your organisation's products or services can be a very powerful and convincing back-up to price-lists or your basic product leaflets or data. The basic principles of the case-study approach are equally applicable in the non-commercial area and the ideas that follow are easily adapted to the promotional needs of a voluntary group. Credibility can be created by simple narrative of facts.

The first stage is to think about the real success stories which have been achieved over the past few months so that you can benefit from what is topical. One of the basic points to consider is summed up admirably by the American marketing commentator Theodore Levitt in a pungent remark in his *The Marketing Mode*: 'Last year one million quarter-inch drills were sold; not because people wanted quarter-inch drills but because they wanted quarter-inch holes.' In other words, a product is sold not so much for its own sake (unless it is some priceless *objet d'art*), but because it satisfies a need. Similarly, the kind of service to the community which fills a gap or solves a problem makes excellent case-study material.

Selecting the best idea
So, what problems have come your way and how has your product or service helped to solve them? Obviously you may not get to know exactly why a customer has bought one of your products or approached the organisation on each particular occasion. But you will usually have a shrewd idea what is involved.

Having picked some ideas for suitable case studies, next try to sort the material information in this way:

1   What is the nature of the problem or need to be satisfied?
2   What particular product or service offered has provided the best solution and given satisfaction?
3   What are the exact features and advantages of this product or service? Are these in any way unique or superior?
4   How was it introduced? Any unique or special aspects of interest?
5   How did it perform?
6   What were the resulting benefits?
7   Any further spin-offs, such as allied areas where similar problems might exist capable of solution in this way?

This, incidentally, is where the fascination of problem-solving through indulging in some lateral thinking merits serious study. Sometimes we can all be rather too limited in our thinking. The real creative skill in marketing, for example, can be to see where additional outlets for the product could exist as a result of proven success.

Probably some of the best ideas will arise from an open discussion with your colleagues. Very often a stunning idea will emerge almost as a throw-away. People are in a special kind of mood where, as the ideas bubble up, the adrenalin starts to flow and they lose inhibitions and the fear of being thought a bit of a nut! It can be an exhilarating and highly creative experience.

Get it down on paper

Once you have accumulated the details of your case study, the copy should be written in a series of short, punchy paragraphs which will follow the sequence suggested above. Use short sentences and avoid jargon. This presentation is not a detailed technical specification but, in a slightly similar way to a press release, a means of attracting someone's interest and creating a willingness to consider your organisation as a strong candidate for satisfying a need or solving a problem. At this stage, decide whether an illustration—a simple diagram or photograph—is necessary by way of further explanation, which will add credibility. Such an illustration could prove a point you are trying to make very effectively.

When all the material is assembled, you will have to decide whether to disclose the name of a particular customer or individual. The answer will depend on the exact nature of your product or service and/or the use to which it is put. If the identity is a material point in the case study, you must be scrupulously careful about approaching the organisation for authorisation and approval of the exact text you propose to use. This is even more important where potentially vulnerable individual people are involved. Some companies are very helpful; others are terrified of seeming to be 'exploited' if they give their blessing or stamp of approval. But if such approval is withheld, the alternative exists of describing the customer circumspectly as, say, 'a medium-sized food-processing company', or whatever is appropriate, so that the reader of the case study will grasp the basic point clearly and be able to relate it to his own situation.

The final stage before actually printing the case study is to set out the text properly on the page. It will probably be necessary to design one or two trial pages to devise a simple yet eye-catching presentation, which is half the battle in gaining interest. The easiest and most effective way is to produce a heading or 'mast-head' for the sheet to give it some kind of identity which is unmistakably your own. Alternatively, the organisation's logo or symbol could be used at the top of the sheet before typing the body of the text below. Something very simple yet effective can be achieved by using transfer print lettering, like Letraset. Try also to think of a short, snappy title which, like the headline of a newspaper column, attracts the reader's attention and gives an idea of the content.

'Quick-print' shops can produce simple leaflets from typewritten originals for what may be a fairly short print run, say fifty or one hundred sheets, a quantity which won't interest a standard printer. The result will be crisper than using a copying machine and the costs are quite modest. The print shop will need a clean, clear original typed with a carbon ribbon from which they can work. Leave a margin of at least $1\frac{1}{2}$in on the left-hand side, use double-spacing and don't crowd the right-hand margin. Avoid indentations of each paragraph, too; provided that each paragraph is clearly separate, this gives an effective businesslike appearance to the typed page. If a golf-ball or daisy-wheel typewriter is used, italics can be sparingly introduced to emphasise a point in the text. Section headings are helpful so that the reader's eye can easily follow through the text.

Before taking the sheet to the printer, check and recheck that the original is absolutely correct in every detail and that no pencilled notes or smudge marks have been left, because modern printing equipment is very accurate and will pick up every blemish. The best way of checking the final copy is to read it out loud (and spell out key names, technical words and figures) to someone else who can follow your draft text and notice any discrepancies or mistakes.

Use a picture

If an illustration is to be used make sure that the photograph 'fits' appropriately into the rest of the material on the page before the text is typed, that it is neither too large nor too small and that it does not overshadow the rest. Probably in this instance an E sized (or 5in × 3½in) print is a good size to show sufficient detail and yet fit on to the page. The exact placing of the photograph should be indicated on the page with light pencil marks so that the text can ride above and below. The photograph can be pasted down on the page after the text and headings have been typed. Quite significant advances have been made in colour photocopying which are worth investigating where very small runs are needed of colour illustrations. If in any doubt, you may wish to consult the print shop beforehand for advice to ensure that the preparation of the original copy is as effective as possible.

Like the measure of attention which a paragraph or two of favourable comment in a newspaper or technical magazine can create, a short selection of case studies can help you considerably. It stimulates attention in a sensible and practical way and it is proof that something of interest and importance has happened. Putting the separate sheets into a plastic wallet or folder adds an effective finishing touch.

Use your press clippings

An equally effective idea is for greater use to be made of press clippings. Don't just file them away. Select half a dozen or so of the most informative press clippings which present your organisation and its activities in the most attractive way. Arrange them carefuly on an A4 sheet, with an appropriate heading—for example, 'In the Public Eye', or 'some recent press coverage of our activities'—in such a way that you can associate them with the name of the publication and when the stories appeared, together with any comment or additional information. Then stick them down ready for photocopying or printing. A good selection of press clippings can provide others with a most authoritative endorsement of what you are doing. As people say, 'if it's in the newspapers, it must be true!' Again, if several sheets are involved, put these into a wallet or folder to aid presentation.

Newsletters

Newsletters or news sheets demand time and effort on the part of a dedicated few but, particularly in the case of voluntary organisations where membership can be diverse and scattered, these can be welcome and effective means of keeping members in touch and informed about activities and the latest developments. At its simplest, the publication can be a single sheet of A4-sized paper, duplicated on both sides, which is pushed through letterboxes by a willing band of helpers or, with adequate funds, it can be a litho-printed four-page small newspaper with photographs. This depends entirely on the needs of the readership, the objectives of the organisation and the money available. Early discussion with printing firms is essential but, in the meantime, there is a wealth of advice primarily aimed at voluntary organisations to be found in an excellent booklet *Making News* (producing a community newspaper) by Barbara Loundes, published by the National Federation of Community Organisations. Whether a parish newsletter, a full-scale community newspaper, a news sheet or a magazine for a company's employees or customers, you must be very clear from the onset why you are producing it, and be capable of ensuring continuity of editorial ideas and enthusiasm, effort and funds—and really make the publication work for its living as a source of lively and worthwhile information.

9
Presentations and Speeches

Many people find public speaking a paralysing and sweat-inducing ordeal but it need not be, provided you are willing to work at it. For good speakers are made not born. You will probably never overcome some nervousness, but preparation and practice will help you to make the most of the occasion. In fact, as most actors will admit, the pre-curtain tension acts as a strange and powerful stimulus; it is the 'couldn't care less' attitude that's the real danger.

An important point to remember, which should give encouragement and confidence, is that there is immense goodwill towards a speaker in an audience. They want you to succeed whether you are making a speech, proposing a vote of thanks or giving a talk or lecture. People want to be entertained or to learn something interesting. If you don't put on a good show, curiously, their embarrassment will quickly turn that goodwill into resentment. So you owe it as much to others as to yourself to learn how to become a better speaker.

What is expected of you?
First, find out as much as you can about the occasion and the audience—what sort of audience and how many? Will women be present? What sort of room? For how long will you be expected to speak? Twenty to thirty minutes should suit most occasions but sometimes, alas, societies expect more from their speakers, perhaps as much as two hours with a break halfway through for refreshments! Will you be expected to answer questions afterwards or will the chairman open up a general discussion? Are copies of your speech or paper needed for printing before the event for distribution afterwards to your audience?

Next, what are you going to say? This is not as difficult as it seems. You have probably been asked to speak because people think you have something interesting to say from your own experience, knowledge and observation. So it is *your* point of view, *your* contribution that they want, not anybody else's.

Gather your material

The first step in the material gathering is to scribble down quickly in any order as many points as you can think of about the subject. The first few will be difficult to formulate but suddenly the ideas will start to flow and you will be agreeably surprised and encouraged. The problem is then to sort out the jumble of notes. The simplest way is to ask yourself 'What is the one vital theme that I want to leave with my audience?' At the start, concentrate on putting one key thought across which opens up your theme. Many people through inexperience make the mistake of bombarding their audience with too many messages too soon and end up by confusing them. The speech should then move logically from that opening thought to others which expand and also reinforce your theme. You should select from your notes the information, facts, quotations and illustrations that support it at each stage of development.

It is probably best to write out what you want to say, since it is the only way of sorting the ideas and making sure that you have done justice to your subject and to your audience. A speech or talk falls naturally into the three parts which Somerset Maugham stipulated for any good short story—beginning, middle and end. So you should try to marshall your material into:

Introduction—your key thought which opens up your theme and an indication of how you will deal with this.
Body—expand on your key thought with supporting information.
Conclusion—summarise.

In other words, 'tell 'em what you're going to tell 'em, tell 'em—and tell 'em what you've told 'em!' And, always, use simple short words, not jargon.

Next, decide what you will speak from. If the subject is very technical, it may be necessary to read the speech word for word, but this is far from satisfactory. It always seems stilted and dull, however well read, and it prevents you from looking at your audience, which is very important. So it is best to speak from a set of notes which you have distilled from your full, written-out version. Never try to memorise the speech—you will probably forget it halfway through and lose your way completely.

Use your notes

Use the outline technique. From your draft make a skeleton or set of notes, setting out each point clearly, thus:

Introduction: the main key to introduce theme—supporting information and indication of the pattern of your presentation (and, in case the chairman hasn't mentioned it, your willingness to take questions at the end).

Body of Speech: (a) Point one
—supporting information
—facts
—illustrations
—examples
(b) Point two (etc, depending upon how many you use) and so on to the conclusion with its crisp set of summary notes.

Putting each part of the speech on to cards the size of a postcard is a good idea. They are a handy size and act as your prompter. Some experienced speakers like to deal with questions from the audience during the presentation, but this is risky and can lead off at a tangent. Except when it is a very informal occasion it is always best to deal with questions afterwards.

Visual aids

Visual aids, such as diagrams or slides, can be very helpful but you need to choose carefully what is suitable to you and your subject. Don't rely on anything which may be too complicated and go berserk on the night. Sometimes the ultra-slick audio-visual show can be counter-productive; it can be so professional as to de-personalise the talk.

People still tend to prefer a presentation which appears to have been prepared specially for them. So, if you feel that visual aids would help to add interest or prove a vital point, until you gain experience you should choose between using a flip-chart or slides on an overhead projector. This means you don't have to darken the room. It is best to produce beforehand, in large capital letters well spaced out on each sheet, the sequence of principal points you are to make, any statistics or other figures, graphs or diagrams you need, and then uncover each sheet as you make your presentation. This can help as a prompt too. Overhead projector slides are special large-sized transparent sheets which are projected onto a screen or a plain, preferably white, wall. You can easily make these beforehand by using coloured-ink pens to illustrate, again, your theme or key points. Alternatively, where tabular matter is involved, if you have access to a photocopying machine you can type out your points in block capitals on plain paper and then insert the transparent sheets into the copier instead of paper to make your transparencies. As you gain experience, you can experiment with different coloured sheets of transparency material to 'jazz up' your slides. These two methods of presentation are the simplest when you have figures or graphs to display. However, don't forget the excellent impact of good 35mm colour transparencies where more detailed illustration is necessary. But don't overdo these and try to use them in a simple sequence. An audience becomes irritated when you are continually turning the lights off and on. With practice, you will soon find out which kind of visual aid suits your subjet and style best.

Making the speech

A comprehensive run-through is vital. Some people go to the extent of using a tape-recording for this. That may be wise because you become used to the sound of your own voice. The first time you try speaking out aloud you may feel unnerved, but confidence comes quickly. The rehearsal should also involve any visual aids.

Using each point in the outline notes as a sort of framework, talk about it, describing the contents of that framework or box in your own words as you would to a friend or colleague. You will find that because you have written it all out beforehand, the material will seem comfortingly familiar. Whether you make a recording or not, time yourself. That can be a salutary experience. You may think you have spoken for twenty minutes, whereas you may find it is nearer forty! If this is the case analyse the notes carefully. Have you included too many illustrations? Could the opening and the close be shorter, crisper? Work at it, not memorising, but becoming familiar and *comfortable* with your material.

On the day, allow sufficient time to arrive at the venue to check the room and to set up and try out your visual aids. If you have rehearsed properly, you will know your material well, but that won't stop you feeling nervous. So, the first thing you do when you get to your feet is to take a deep breath and look right around your audience. Don't rush into your speech. Being deliberate in this way seems to establish a helpful bond with the audience and also gives you a chance to gather your wits together. Start to speak slowly and clearly. Don't shout but make sure that your voice is carrying well throughout the audience. If the people in the last row appear to be straining to hear you, raise your voice a little until they seem comfortable. 'Vary the pitch and vary the pace' was Lloyd George's advice to the young Harold Macmillan before his maiden speech to the Commons. If you are faced with a microphone, make sure before you start that it is at the right height for you and approximately a foot away from your mouth—and then forget it!

Even if you are not a very fluent speaker you will get your audience's interest and support if you speak crisply and sincerely. Don't begin your speech, 'When I was asked to make this speech I wondered what on earth I could say', and don't use a 'blue' joke at any time! Humour is more difficult to use well in a speech than you might imagine. If a really funny story or personal anecdote seems to fit in naturally and you feel at ease telling it, then use it. But don't drag in a story by the scruff of its neck just for the sake of it.

Once you have started, you will find that you will relax considerably and get into your stride because you are talking about a familiar subject to people who will be interested to hear your particular slant or viewpoint. If you feel like using your hands to underline a point as you might in an ordinary conversation, then do so. Exaggerated, wide, sweeping gestures may alarm the audience nearest to you but a few restrained ones can be most effective. Don't jingle the coins in your pocket or keep fingering any pieces of jewellery. But above all, look at your audience; eye contact is most important. Staring down fixedly at your notes is bad. If you imagine that you are talking to individuals scattered at different points about the audience, turning towards them as you talk, it helps.

The close of your speech is important. Watch the time and don't overrun so that you have to gabble to a hurried conclusion. If possible it is a good idea, where there is no clock visible on the wall, to take your watch off and place it where you can see it as you speak. After you have made your summing up, just nod your head, smile and then sit down. There is no need to thank the audience. If you have done the job well, it is up to them to thank you. But if there is someone who has been particularly helpful to you in the organisation of the function, find a spot in your speech to say thank you.

10
Conferences

Planning a seminar, 'teach-in' or conference is something that needs a blend of imagination, determination, patience and a fastidious attention to detail. Once enthusiasm for the idea of holding a conference has gathered momentum, there are some vital questions to be asked before you start to make all the arrangements.

A conference will involve a considerable number of people and will divert their attention and effort from day-to-day responsibilities. Even the most modest get-together can cost a surprisingly large amount of money. Are you really sure that it is the best way of achieving your objective? Wouldn't some other medium be better? Provided, however, there is a clearly identified and promoted theme, a conference is a splendid way of giving information and exchanging ideas on a subject of common interest, as well as creating enthusiasm. The personal contact is worth a very great deal, particularly where people would not normally have the chance of meeting each other.

Provided the right location is chosen with the most suitable facilities, there is nothing like a conference away from offices, plants and the routine of everyday existence to get full involvement and commitment. Convenient though it may be to hold such a conference in your own town or on your own premises, the delegates tend to appear and disappear with vague excuses, if only to prove how indispensable they are elsewhere. If the conference is on an important theme or where a great deal of input is required by way of discussion or in study groups, provided the budget will allow or the event can be self-financing, a mid-week or weekend residential conference can produce immediate and longer-lasting results.

Size, time and location
The size of a conference is immensely important. Big convention-style 'bun fights' are old hat today, except in politics, showbiz or the motor-car industry. To achieve maximum involvement and

participation, thirty to forty people is about the wisest upper limit. After the formal presentations, setting the scene, planting the thoughts and stirring up the ideas, you want lively discussion and question-and-answer sessions. Large audiences stay as large audiences rather then becoming cohesive groups of participating delegates. Another problem which must be overcome early in the planning stage is to decide who is eligible to attend the conference. This has an important bearing on the resources, the style and the facilities needed.

The ideal time to hold a conference is an off-peak moment in the calendar but any attempt to find the perfect moment in the year may be just wishful thinking. Though weekend conferences are attractive to avoid cutting into the working week, these may be unfair to wives and families. Before coming to any hard and fast conclusion deciding on the exact length it is best to study the conference content first.

The secret is to try to find a conference setting that combines comfort with simplicity, good facilities with agreeable surroundings. Schools and universities out of term offer excellent facilities today and make a pleasant change from standardised hotels. They are very well equipped with all the latest communication aids, which help to give a conference a professional style. Alternatively, the choice of a conveniently located, traditional yet discreetly modernised country hotel may be a suitable setting.

Establish a realistic budget at an early stage. Particularly if sponsorship is involved in providing funds, the budget proposals must be detailed and thorough.

When all the preliminary thinking has been done, one person should be appointed with complete responsibility for organising and supervising the conference. That organiser should be quite divorced from any executive part of the programme so that he or she can offer objective help and comment.

Check the facilities

It is vital that the intended location is visited to check the facilities in detail. It is surprising what horrors can emerge which, if not checked and rectified well ahead of time, could ruin the whole event: for example, meeting-rooms without sound-proofing or adequate ventilation, overlooking busy highways, or conflicting events already booked at the hotel which may divert hotel staff's attention away from delegates' needs.

Obviously the focal point of a successful conference must be a first-rate chairman, but as far as the content of the conference is concerned, plenty of time must be allowed to be sure of attracting the preferred speakers. In the detailed planning of the programme, even though the conference may be on one theme, variety is the spice of life and it is essential that enough time is left for discussion in each session.

Another factor is pinning speakers down to agree their exact topic (and prepare their visual aids) well in advance so that there is no danger of duplication or unfortunate clash of interest. That is almost as difficult as getting them to put their material down on paper. Certainly the most effective way of covering much ground in a short time is for circulation of the conference papers well in advance of the event, with crisp summaries on the day by the speakers. That allows for plenty of participation from the delegates. The thorough pre-briefing of conference delegates well before they arrive is immensely important. Telling them, too, whether or not the conference will be informal is a helpful pointer for what they may choose to wear, and if there is to be a formal dinner to open or close the conference whether dinner jackets are required for the men.

How do you judge the success of a conference? F. Scott-Fitzgerald declared 'No grand idea was ever born in a conference, but a lot of foolish ideas have died there.' More practically, every delegate attending should be asked to comment on a special form about a week after the event has ended and to offer suggestions for improvements. That allows time for reflection and any post-conferential euphoria to evaporate.

11
Personal Communication

Effective communication is an important means of getting people to work together more harmoniously and encourages greater involvement and commitment. The Americans use the expression 'talk with' which implies a willingness to engage in dialogue rather than just talk at or to someone. The need to listen is all too often forgotten when putting our point of view or message across.

The right attitude

Successful communication begins with the right attitude of mind of the boss as leader of the team. The purpose and objectives of the organisation should be clear cut in his or her mind, but it is vital that this certainty of aim and purpose is clear to everyone else. That may seem obvious, yet it takes time and determination to ensure that everybody is on the right wavelength—and stays there. Naturally, there will be individual differences of opinion but the general 'climate of opinion' should be such that these differences can be accommodated, indeed focused creatively on your own thinking as the leader.

The next most vital point is to ensure that people are clear about the exact nature of their job or function, what is expected of them and what they can expect in return. This means a clear delineation of their responsibilities and also the realisation of the significance of their role; in other words, what happens to the products being made or the worth to others of the service provided. Not offering these essentials means that other efforts to keep people in the picture will be ineffective expedients.

Paper-work

In a small organisation you can certainly use paper to help face-to-face communication efforts. For example, if you receive an interesting letter from a satisfied customer or someone your organisation has helped, why not pin a copy on your notice-board? A letter of praise used in this way can give a marvellous fillip to morale. Notice-boards are valuable communication aids but do make sure they look attractive, are well positioned and properly maintained. Make it someone's particular responsibility to look after them. Nothing looks worse than a notice-board with age-old bits of paper attracting more and more dust. Often it is better to have a blank notice-board after the particular notice has served its purpose and is removed. Then, when something new comes along, it is seen to be 'news'.

Everyone in the organisation should be familiar with any promotional or technical literature it publishes, even if their job is not strictly related to the publicity function. Every member of an organisation should be able to talk knowledgeably about latest developments. A casual conversation in a pub or on holiday could lead to a useful new opportunity.

Face-to-face briefing

But the printed word is a poor second to the chance of talking *with* people, giving them the opportunity to share in the information and to ask questions. Just in the same way that time is set aside for training, it is essential to have full-scale briefings of the whole team at regular intervals. Exactly what those intervals are must be decided by the nature of the business or activity, but these should not be less than quarterly for general background information. The Industrial Society, supported by both industry and the trade unions, has done much to promote the practice of team briefing and recommends the four Ps format for each session: Progress (achievements, results plus significant trends or problems); People (what's happening to whom); Policy (changes of objective, priority or method); and, very important, Points of Action (with clear responsibility for these), plus the chance for people to join in with discussion, ideas and questions. There will, of course, be plenty of occasions when something important crops up needing urgent discussion and attention—a quality problem, a difficult customer, a financial crisis, a change of work routine—when you may need people to come together on an *ad hoc* basis. (If there are problems or difficulties which relate to individuals, you must sort these out beforehand.)

Assembling your team when there is something of interest and importance to say actually saves time. Leaving everything to chance in the hope that the message will filter through to all concerned is not facing up to your responsibility as leader of the company. A briefing note or a notice-board bulletin can always be used as written confirmation of a verbal briefing.

Proper briefing sessions are just as relevant to a team of helpers in a charity or any other voluntary group where people have to work together effectively to achieve a programme or a target. They need and like to be 'in the know' just as much as employees in a factory. Indeed, it may be more difficult for voluntary helpers because they may work in isolation or attend at odd times when they have little chance of meeting many others in the organisation. People's leisure time is precious, but if such briefings are positive and well run, the opportunity to hear things at first hand will be appreciated.

Open days

Another opportunity to improve communication in a small company is the occasional open day for employees and their families. Regardless of the size or nature of the company, open days are a very effective and direct way of bridging any gulf between family and workplace. The hard work and time involved are more than repaid in the interest and pride which are created by throwing open the doors to employees' families and friends.

Perhaps the most important factor in arranging this sort of function, apart from fixing a realistic budget, picking the right day and establishing a small lively organising committee, is to make the day seem as informal as possible. It is a day for people to show off *their* organisation. Therefore in a factory, for example, there should be as few restrictions as possible within the normal, sensible precautions of commercial security and personal safety. That means making sure everything is right behind the scenes and avoiding any suggestion that people are being guided round their own organisation! You may have to provide discreet reminders by plotting out a clear route to be followed with plenty of detail as to what goes on in each department and why. Rather than 'guides' have 'hosts', clearly labelled so that they can answer questions.

It is very important to have just the right amount of activity or things to be looked at on an open day. Children, of course, can be a hazard on such occasions but the route can be restricted in such a way that likely dangers are bypassed. The 'hosts' or marshals must also be asked to keep a wary eye on them. To avoid possible embarrassment try to find out whether any of your visitors are disabled and make arrangements accordingly.

It is necessary to tell people about the actual event in plenty of time on notice-boards and via any other convenient medium, such as bulletins or employees' wage packets. Nearer the time, it is important to have a rough idea of actual numbers so that detailed catering arrangements can be made and tickets issued which also have a section on them to be given up in exchange for refreshments.

Although on these occasions the employees or voluntary helpers are the real VIPs, an open day can be a useful opportunity to invite a number of people who have a special relationship with the organisation, such as important suppliers, local dignatories, police, fire-service representatives—and friendly journalists. But there should be no form of demarcation between one type of visitor and another during the function—no special marquee or private refreshment area. If it is appropriate to provide some special kind of entertainment for important visitors, this should be provided either before or after the event, for instance a lunch at a local hotel. Some of the most appreciative special visitors to such a function are probably pensioned employees, or former members or helpers. Their obvious pleasure and pride at being remembered is a salutary experience. Pay particular attention to the welcome that people receive on arrival. You as boss or organiser must be very much in evidence.

Prepare an attractive handout sheet giving information about the organisation: when it was established, the products or services offered and types of customer. It will be a useful publicity aid.

Special visitors
A final word of advice on handling 'special' visitors. If by hard work, good management or sheer good luck you are picked out for a visit by a very important VIP, whose 'star' rating may range from a show-bizz personality or government minister to royalty, always *immediately* seek the very best advice, allowing as much time as possible to implement that advice, to check and recheck details of the programme and premises, and brief and rehearse those involved. That means seeking the advice not only of officials but of other firms or organisations which have already had such visits. Where royalty or government VIPs are concerned, security matters are so delicate and vital that you will be carefully vetted on several occasions and be helped in the course of such visitations with detailed advice. These occasions will demand much time and inevitably some additional expense but the benefits in terms of a fillip to morale and public acclaim will be priceless.

12
Exhibitions

Taking part in any exhibition or public display can be a hard and expensive slog with few obvious benefits, a morale-boosting success or an utter flop. Yet at the right moment in an organisation's career or the life of a product, if you don't stand in the market place and shout about your wares a vital opportunity may be missed. There is a fair chance that if you can persuade a particular buyer to come along to see you in a different setting, you may get him in a more mellow and friendly mood out of his office. There is always the chance of grabbing the attention of someone you would never have any hope of meeting on any other occasion. A company must rely on tough commercial principles in deciding whether or not to exhibit.

But if you are running a voluntary organisation, different considerations may arise. You may be offered free space. You may be invited to share a multiple stand with kindred bodies. Even so, there will be a number of 'hidden' costs which must be carefully studied before committing yourself. The Incorporated Society of British Advertisers (ISBA) in an excellent booklet, *Guide to Industrial Publicity*, lists six vital questions to be answered before you take the plunge. They are of equal relevance to businessmen or to voluntary helpers:

1 Are your customers, or potential customers, likely to attend the exhibition on a reasonable scale? This question may seem obvious, but it is remarkable how often it cannot possibly have been answered correctly.
2 On what scale is it necessary for you to take part, ie the size of the stand, location and type of stand and the exhibits themselves? This will govern the total cost.
3 Can you comply with the regulations, or are there conditions you will find it hard to meet?
4 Can you afford it—or even if you can, would the money be better spent in another medium?
5 Can you staff your exhibit without completely dislocating your other commitments?

6   Are you able and prepared to handle quickly all the enquiries on your stand during the exhibition or immediately afterwards?

If you do decide to take part in a particular exhibition, it is important not to overlook the full public relations aspects of such an exercise. In all the hard work and frenzy, it is easy to forget that there are some important PR techniques, particularly in your relations with the press, which can earn extra publicity mileage. Contact with the press must be high up on a list of planning priorities.

Involve the press

Today, more and more press coverage of exhibitions is being handled by the trade, technical and other specialist magazines in preliminary reports of what is going to happen rather than a review of the exhibition once it has opened—though, with luck, they may do both. However, if you can get a good mention in the advance publicity, it may help attract visitors and potential customers to your stand.

It is wise to check with the exhibition organisers what their own press information service is likely to be in advance of the opening, and to make sure that your organisation's name and exhibit will be included in the pre-exhibition release—and then, as a belt and braces operation, make sure that you send your own release out in plenty of time to those publications which you know are keenly studied by your target publics. This may seem like duplication but you want to make sure that you are not overlooked. That can happen in the flurry of paper that surrounds a major promotional event like an exhibition. With care and a little luck, you can ensure that a busy journalist puts your name down on the list of stands he intends to visit.

So, with the advance press information, think very carefully about the key features of what you are going to exhibit, whether there is something of unusual interest on the stand or, if there is not a genuinely 'newsworthy' story in this, give a short, punchy résumé of your activities and achievements and how this exhibition matches your objectives and plans. This could just fit into a journalist's framework of tackling the exhibition in a feature article. But make sure that what you write is crisp and to the point (remember the formula: What? Who? Where? When? How? Why?). Don't forget to mention your stand number and its precise location, if necessary.

When it comes to the actual exhibition, it is a good idea to prepare a digest or bulletin rather than a press release. This document is possibly more versatile when budgets are slim because it can be used for the press and also for other interested people who visit your stand, to supplement the existing range of brochures and catalogues. Pick out the highlights and, again, write about them briefly and factually.

Add some photos

Make sure that you have a selection of good photographs available to offer a journalist who visits your stand. If your budget is really tight, make sure that you have one good, recently taken shot of the item or theme you are emphasising on your stand. The pictures you give to magazines may not be used immediately, but can be filed by editors for future use. Although this might seem an unjustified extra expense, such a photograph can also then be used for your next publicity leaflet. It is a question, again, of thinking ahead and making sure that your promotional material is as versatile as possible.

Time, as well as money, will be fully stretched, but if you're committed to exhibit, you must do the job properly. So, about ten days before the exhibition opens, make a point of picking out those magazines you consider absolutely vital to your operation. Then telephone the editor and invite him personally (or any of his colleagues covering the exhibition) to visit your stand, pointing out very specifically what they will see of interest there. Sometimes this makes all the difference to the press when deciding which stands to visit. Don't forget to brief your own colleagues so that if you are not there at the particular moment the journalist turns up, he or she can be treated with the importance of a customer. Indeed, the journalist *is* a customer—for information about your activities. Also, make sure there is a small supply of your visiting cards on the stand so that, again, if you are not around, the journalist knows how to get in touch with you. Never forget the opportunities that always exist for getting extra publicity by making sure that, in addition to the specialist press, you alert your local newspaper and radio station, even if you are exhibiting away from your home base.

Look out for TV

Keep a keen eye open, too, during the exhibition for roving TV journalists and cameramen. Usually they are attracted by something moving on a stand, for obvious reasons. But before the opening day, make a point of finding out from the exhibition organisers what arrangements they have made for TV coverage and see how you can join in. Exhibition press rooms are usually chaotic, however well organised the exhibition itself may be. There is so much paper around that it is a matter of luck whether or not your own information or very existence is noted by a busy journalist. After the exhibition because not every journalist you would wish to meet manages to go to the exhibition, it is wise to send the press material direct to the magazine.

Always be optimistic, having taken the plunge. Perhaps a journalist, radio or TV reporter with attendant cameramen will appear on your stand and be genuinely interested in what you are showing. Perhaps you will be able to announce an interesting order or achievement during the exhibition and so take advantage of the organisers' free publicity machine. On such occasions the media loves good news stories.

13
Other PR Opportunities

Secondary channels for getting publicity are perhaps not as immediate as favourable coverage in a newspaper or magazine, or on TV and radio. Yet, who knows when you may need help from your MP, local councillor, head of a professional body or institute, or other official? Also, there are such steps as writing letters to the newspaper or radio, or taking part in 'phone-in programmes on the subject which is your major concern. But it needs luck as well as patience. It may be some time before a suitable programme is broadcast and, in any case, the producer may not take your question to the experts in the studio.

These opportunities, however, are dependent on either a well-written letter or an effective telephone call.

A well-written letter is essential
Considering the number of letters most of us write and receive every week, it is rather disturbing that so few are attractive, persuasive or even interesting. That is why so many go into the waste-paper basket or are pushed to one side in the hope of finding time later to deal with them. But a properly constructed letter is vital if you are making an initial contact with an MP or any official. (The same, of course, applies with letters to customers or suppliers, or the bank manager.) Usually, we rush the job by not collecting our thoughts together beforehand or by dictating a letter off the cuff to a secretary or a machine. Many letters are badly constructed, too long and impersonal. The guiding principle is that all such letters should be brief, to the point, yet contain something of the writer's individuality. Most people hide themselves behind jargon and verbosity, using language they would never dream of using in any face-to-face contact. As with press releases, the structure and style of a letter are everything. Using simple direct words, you must attract attention in your opening paragraphs and at the same time establish credibility by making it clear why you feel you have a genuine need as an individual or representative of an organisa-

tion to be noticed or helped. A long, rambling letter to a newspaper correspondence column will either be cut to ribbons or, most likely, thrown away. A harrassed MP tackling his correspondence after an all-night sitting in the House, won't be impressed by a semi-legible jumble concluded by an indecipherable signature. So, wherever possible, all important letters, whether to the press or to an MP or official, should be typed (and a copy kept), and then signed above the typed writer's name and designation. Just as you must make it clear who and what you are, so you should ensure that you spell your intended recipient's name correctly and use his or her title and the correct name and address of the organisation, as appropriate. Be direct, but always polite, in print. It is not a bad idea where a great deal hangs on that letter to do a careful draft first and then ask someone to read it. If you write in a hurry, or in anger, you may make a stupid mistake or, worse, a most damaging statement.

The successful 'phone call
Usually, an approach to someone like an MP or a senior official in a government department or on your local council, is best made by letter first and then followed up by a telephone call. That is why telephone calls can be crucial too. The telephone is a curious instrument. It can be your ally or your enemy. It can be an invaluable bridge between two people or an appalling communications barrier. Most 'phone calls, alas, are not particularly memorable experiences, but when they are, you find yourself warming to the unseen caller. Some people seem to be able to be both friendly and persuasive on the telephone, so it is worth taking time and trouble to learn some of their basic techniques.

Before you make an important telephone call, jot down the main points you wish to convey. Ask yourself what you hope to achieve from the call. Always make sure you know to whom you are talking and that the other person knows who you are. Identification is vital. Give your own full name and ask his or her's. Don't rush into what you have to say, but carefully establish the basic territory that lies between you. Speak clearly and try to put a little 'colour' into your voice in the same way you would if you were actually talking to the person in the same room. You can obtain a most sympathetic response if you come across as an individual, on the line. Say what you have to say as concisely as possible, and always take care to listen carefully to the other person's replies. Sound interesting and interested. If possible, always try to create a bond of mutual interest so that it is easier to reach agreement either in arranging a meeting or in taking some appropriate action. Be persuasive but not 'pushy' and don't attempt to drag the conversation out when it is clearly at an end. It is better to make another call on another day.

Most members of Parliament are conscientious and approachable people who care about helping their constituents. But most are very overworked. They appreciate those who show some consideration by not bombarding them with trivia. They appreciate, even more, efforts to keep them in the picture with concise letters or briefing notes on a matter which can be seen to be of mutual concern, and where an MP's action or support can make all the difference between success or failure. Provided plenty of notice is given, a personal invitation to your MP to attend an important function put on by your organisation is appreciated and may remove all kinds of obstacles. When writing to MPs, send your letter to their constituency addresses, with a copy to them at the House of Commons, to be sure of reaching them. Once you have established contact by letter, it is that much easier to telephone. The telephone number of the House of Commons is (01) 219 3000. Once you get through, you may find the MP has an individual number in the House, or messages can be left for MPs on (01) 219 4343.

The same principles apply when contacting officials or your local councillor. Write first, then telephone to follow up an important matter, or seek help or advice. With officialdom be firm but always polite and to the point. Local councillors are often most anxious to help you. But don't risk trying their patience and goodwill by bothering them with inessentials. Reserve for them important issues that really matter but, as with MPs, try to establish a personal link by keeping them fully informed on what you are trying to do. If they recognise you as a responsible individual, then you and your organisation are more likely to win their willing support.

Correspondence columns
Letters to the correspondence columns of newspapers and other publications can be a useful opportunity for gaining attention and support. Many radio and television programmes also run their own correspondence columns. But always have something interesting to say and be brief. Convey the point you want to

make in the first couple of sentences in simple, punchy language. Observe deadlines: with daily newspapers make sure your letter is received by the morning of the day before publication. You can either sign the letter, which should always be typed, preferably in double-spaced lines, as an individual member of your organisation or you can obtain additional signatures. But always type out the names, otherwise the letter won't be used. Be prepared to see your letter drastically sub-edited and in some cases even rewritten for the sake of clarity and conciseness! Try to read the local newspapers regularly. You can often spot an issue or event which you can use as an opportunity for a follow-up letter or comment from your viewpoint or organisation.

'On the air'

Almost every radio and TV station now has 'phone-ins, audience participations and what are called 'access' programmes, where the lucky few who have a really good idea are actually given air time, with professional assistance, to put together their own programme. These opportunities should certainly be considered but the chances of your group acquiring its own programme are usually slim. You are much more likely to have the chance to take part in one of the many 'phone-ins on radio. Blatant promotion for a product or a cause may not get past the production team. But if you have an interesting topical point to make, or a piece of information which makes a contribution to the programme's theme, there is a good chance you'll be invited to go on the air. Once you are in direct contact with the production unit, make sure you listen carefully to their technical instructions, such as not trying to listen to yourself on a radio in the same room while you're on the telephone. Be sure beforehand what points you want to make and say them clearly and concisely, but don't solemnly read these out because they will sound stilted and insincere.

With each of these extra opportunities for putting your point of view directly, you have to learn to compete with everyone else trying to gain access to individuals and audiences who might be of help. Yet if you do succeed in attracting attention, other events may follow. A journalist may want to interview you for a fuller story. Listeners, or readers, may be persuaded to contact you. With enough appearances on local radio or TV you (or someone in your organisation) may become the accepted local expert on a specialist subject and find your services in great demand.

14
Fund Raising and Sponsorship

Voluntary organisations spend an important slice of their time raising funds to finance their activities. Such funds may be modest in relation to their aims and objectives, or may be the sole justification for their existence. But money is needed either way and even small companies will find themselves being approached with increasing frequency. So, a brief comment on fund raising and sponsorship is appropriate.

An approach to any statutory body, organisation, trust, philanthropic body or company to ask for money is often a delicate and difficult task which demands both imagination and patience. Imagination is needed because of the great number of badly conceived, impractical and undiplomatic approaches made every day of the year by people who have not taken the time or trouble to do any elementary research into the feasibility of funds being available from a particular body. Patience is also a much-needed attribute because there are seldom any quick favourable results. After an initial letter of acknowledgement, if you are lucky, you must expect to wait many weeks before you know of success or failure. Most money-dispensing organisations have to plan well ahead and may only make decisions on how to spend their money at quarterly or half-yearly meetings. Some respond quickly to an urgent approach if the venture is attractive and worthwhile, but they form the minority. Some money-seeking organisations depend for their research on that bible, *Directory of Grant-Making Trusts*, compiled and published by the Charities Aid Foundation, but usually available in reference libraries, which lists all the charities and trusts in the UK with details of terms of reference, aims and objectives. Having extracted the names of those which seem nearest their own aims, they will then mail letters to each. This grape-shot approach today is seldom effective. It is far better to be selective and personal in your approach. Personal introductions to named individuals in an organisation who are known to have influence on funds are desirable. These people may be a company secretary or a director with known philanthropic leanings or social awareness, or a good public relations officer.

The key element in a personal approach of any kind is to try to establish at the earliest stage any common ground of mutual concern and interest. That body or company may be anxious to spend its money in a particular year in a way which does not follow the usual pattern of previous years. For example, a company may have decided to reduce support for national charities and concentrate on helping local ventures which have some connection with its own local factories or branches. So, try to find a way in which your needs can match theirs. Most companies like to feel that their charitable donations are 'cost effective' in the sense that they will be used efficiently in the cause of something with which they can identify.

Another trend in fund raising is to identify certain specifics which can be supported. Some companies may not be willing to donate a sum of money to the general funds of an organisation. Instead, they may be persuaded to finance a particular activity. For example, they will provide money or services to cover the printing of stationery, literature, event or exhibition programmes and catalogues, accommodation or items of equipment. So again, it is important to know what to ask for which fits in with the thinking and wishes of an individual company.

Always seek expert advice in your fund-raising activity. Most people have learnt invaluable lessons from previous fund raising experiences. In a number of local authorities, a charities' advisory officer may have been appointed to give advice on how to try to find your way through a massive tangle of trusts and other charitable organisations—and to ensure that there is as little duplication of effort as possible in any locality. An interview with an officer could increase your chances of success.

The Charity Commission

The charities' advisory officer may be able to advise you on whether your own organisation should seek charitable status. Such a decision is crucial and needs to be taken with the very best advice. The Charity Commission, established in 1853, is a rather formidable body with whom over 140,000 charities are registered. Besides maintaining the official register, the commissioners promote the effective use of funds raised, hold (in the hands of an official custodian) investments made by charities and remit the income to them. The commissioners administer the law relating to charities. The main benefit of this law is to confer upon charities tax repayments, particularly as a result of donations made under covenant.

To qualify as a charity, an organisation must not be involved in any political activity but must be seen clearly to carry out works that are to the public good. This must be remembered in the drafting of any constitution which has to be submitted to the Charity Commission to consider your organisation's status. Obtain good advice in the drafting of this vital document, and then once your application has gone in to the commissioners, be prepared for a long wait. They are infinitely vigilant and discriminating of the many submissions made each year.

Sponsorship

In contrast to the drudgery and heartache of conventional fund raising, sponsorship nowadays has acquired all the glitter and glamour of a showbiz activity. It is big business with a proliferating bevy of specialist companies, all willing to give expert advice on how to match needs with resources. Around £60 million a year is now spent by companies in sponsoring events, competitions, personalities and teams. In 1971 that figure was £16 million. Today the lion's share of sponsorship money (well over £20 million) goes towards sports sponsorship, but sponsorship of the arts has also shown a very healthy growth and is now over £13 million per annum. There have been significant changes in sponsorship as a result of legislation and attitude. With the government ban on TV cigarette advertising and the outlawing of any other advertising connection with health or sport, many tobacco companies have moved into sports sponsorship to return to the public eye. Industry has become much more aware of the benefits arising from arts sponsorship. The influence of the Association of Business Sponsorship of the Arts (ABSA) has been considerable in encouraging sponsorship of the arts by individual companies. Indeed, it is now a recognised form of modern patronage which, with certain qualifications, is tax effective and a useful part of any public relations programme.

How you look at sponsorship depends on whether you are the sponsor or the sponsored. Some companies may have been frightened off by the mistaken belief that large sums are necessary to achieve worthwhile results. That is certainly not the case and a very small investment spent with care and imagination which links in with your total public relations effort can produce gratifying results. Arranging for the company's name on the T-shirt worn by a celebrity in a sponsored walk, or providing flags or labelled barrier ropes at a public event can put you cheaply in the public eye.

Sponsorship of any kind by a small company must be a hard-nosed decision with clear and commercial objectives, such as winning greater recognition in its locality or for its products, as well as an act of good neighbourliness. It must fit topically into the company's own aims and style of operation. It is no use pretending that some attractive form of sponsorship will persuade others to believe you are something you are not. It may not achieve exactly the results you are looking for the first time you do it, so arranging to sponsor an event for two or three years running may be worth considering. This may give you the chance to play a part in improving the actual event so that even closer identification is possible with the company. It is better to stick to one type of sponsorship and do it well than spread limited funds too thinly over several events. A vital component in successful sponsorship is commitment from both the sponsor and the sponsored recipient. It must be seen as a realistic working relationship or partnership of mutual benefit. Both sides must have clear ideas from the onset about what each can gain. There are always a number of 'extras' or hidden costs, such as executive time, transport or printing costs, and there may be unforeseen but necessary last-minute changes to the events or activity being sponsored. So, as well as a tight discipline over financial matters, some wise flexibility may be required.

Approaching a sponsor

The English Tourist Board in an excellent document *The Give and Take of Sponsorship* has listed twenty points to take into account when approaching a potential sponsor:

1 The presentation must be clearly typed and addressed in person. If the name of the person responsible for sponsorship is not known, telephone the company secretary and ask.

2 Never submit duplicated letters, either with or without a duplicated signature. Such letters have little hope of having their request taken further.

3 In the case where a conglomerate company has branches in the region, it is advisable to make contact and discuss the project at regional level first. Having won over the regional officer they, in turn, can give an advantageous report to the headquarters.

4 Companies have been known to sponsor an activity because the 'Chairman is a great golfer, musician,' etc. Know the Chairman's hobbies.

5 Is there a connection between the potential sponsor and the activity?

6 The applicant should give full details of the organisation he represents.

7 Include details of the financial viability of both the applicant and the project.

8 Give a detailed description of the anticipated event.

9 Send back-up documents such as feasibility studies, budget forecasts, etc. where available.

10 Indicate type of market the sponsor is likely to reach.

11 Explain whether the activity will have national or local appeal.

12 Has the quality of the event been clarified and is the event appropriate to the sponsor's type of business?

13 List the possible benefits to the sponsor.

14 Is there likely to be any impact on the sponsor's business?

15 Are there likely to be any on-going benefits to the sponsor after the event?

16 Are the sponsor's staff likely to benefit or become involved?

17 Tell the companies whether any other companies have been, or are to be, approached and, if so, what results were obtained.

18 The willingness to acknowledge a company's product may be an advantage but is not necessarily a condition of support.

19 Be prepared to alter the name of the event to suit the sponsor or create an event that fits both the company's and the applicant's objectives.

20 The applicant must be realistic in his requests.

The same document also gives much valuable information about charities and covenants and lists many sources of additional advice.

Despite the problems of industry, unemployment and new stresses and strains felt by the welfare state, there are plenty of opportunities to establish new relationships and understanding between the worlds of leisure and work which can enrich both. Giving and receiving funds, sponsoring and being sponsored, can be a vital and interesting part of such a link but it needs realism and discipline as well as benevolence. If successful, it can bring great satisfaction as well as being a means of creating a little fun in our lives.

15
Altogether Now

Whether you are large or small as a business, whether you deal in industrial products or consumer goods, whether you are a voluntary group or sports club, *response* is a vital quality. In the same way that a good part of being an effective individual is a capacity to listen to other people, to take note of their ideas and feelings, so when you deal with customers or people in need of help, you must be constantly alert to their needs and wishes.

Response means the speed and manner in which an organisation reacts to people who make contact whether by letter, telephone or in person. It takes no more time or cost to be courteous, welcoming and helpul than it takes to be rude, thoughtless or inefficient. Actually repairing the damage caused by dissatisfied customers can be much more time-consuming *and* unprofitable. A courteous approach and a helpful attitude can be a very sound investment for long-term success. So first, by setting the right example, make sure that every single person in your company believes in the reality of the customer or the 'client' by briefing and educating your staff about how your products are sold and used, or the full range of services and facilities available to the community.

Whether a small business or a voluntary group, deal with telephone calls and correspondence promptly and intelligently. Make it a firm 'rule of the house' that your response is quick and courteous. If the whole matter cannot be settled there and then, a preliminary telephone call is made or letter written of acknowledgement and explanation with the promise of settling the matter as quickly as possible, *which is kept.* People are quite happy to wait a reasonable time provided they are confident they are not ignored or forgotten.

Of course, things will go wrong—and knowing how to put matters right is as important as trying to ensure that they don't go wrong in the first place. Knowing when and how to apologise is crucial. That does not mean being feeble or compliant; quite the reverse. It often takes courage and the swallowing of your pride to admit you are wrong and that you mean to put matters right as quickly and fairly as possible.

It is wise to establish a proper complaints procedure which is both just and effective. The exact details will depend very much on the nature of your product or the activities of your organisation. But speed is of the essence. Very often the offer of a token credit towards the purchase of the next item, a free service, or a well-written letter of apology works wonders. It may even turn someone all set to involve the Press or the local Consumers Advisory Office into an ally. By all means satisfy yourself that the complaint is genuine and reasonable, but do that quickly instead of trying to kid yourself that if you wait then maybe the disgruntled customer will tire and retreat.

Another essential part of good business or social behaviour is knowing when to say 'thank you'. Criticism, too often, is the rule and praise the exception. It must be another 'rule of the house' that thanks are given promptly whenever someone has done their job well or made an extra effort. A word of thanks either verbally or in a letter, is a splendid morale booster: speakers at your conference, a special visitor, a supplier who has made that extra effort to deliver something ahead of schedule so you can solve an unforeseen problem. Saying 'thank you' gives the reassurance that the extra effort is appreciated. Some people find it very difficult to give thanks and praise. Equally, some people can appear to be very embarrassed on the receiving end. But persevere, because it pays dividends. Courtesy, as well as a lubricant which eases business practice and social relationships, is a sign of sincerity and people will come to trust you and think well of you. It is a special kind of credit. But it is not proof against devaluation.

Like responsive business behaviour, good PR has to be worked for and maintained with care. It doesn't just 'happen'. You cannot just assemble all the components, give them a shake or two and then observe some magical coherent pattern before you. Luck sometimes does play a part in providing an exceptionally newsworthy story, but it is foolish to rely absolutely on its presence. Public relations is a crucial part of the overall management of any worthwhile project or enterprise. As with sound financial control, technical service or the marketing of a product, public relations merits the attention and involvement of those who lead a team in an organisation even though the carrying out of a programme may be a delegated responsibility. Effective and efficient PR is the result of the careful planning of a detailed programme which can be monitored during its progress, if necessary being adjusted to suit changing circumstances or sudden developments and then honestly evaluated at the close. It depends on having the right attitude towards other people and the outside world. A genuine interest in what makes PR 'tick' and an intelligent observation of what other companies and organisations do are vital elements if you want to gain experience, confidence and develop your own resources. Perhaps, like the plots of the world's great works of fiction or drama, there is a surprisingly small number of new, totally original PR ideas. The skill lies in the way in which we can work on these to develop or adapt them for our own purposes. This is the challenge, excitement and creativity of good PR.

There are five essential steps in designing an effective course of PR action. First, you must establish your policy and define your objectives as a result of identifying the target audiences with which you need to communicate. Second, you specify the action to be taken through listing the various appropriate components, whether by use of the press or direct personal contact. Third, you build up the programme with a logical and realistic timetable which, depending on the type of organisation and its objectives, may either start with a headline-grabbing launch or on an altogether quieter level as a modest lead from which interest and support are patiently developed so that you hopefully can finish on a high sustained note of success. Fourth, you establish a sensible budget which you can afford and to which you can stick. Fifth, you must take care to assess the progress of the programme at various stages and at its close.

Because budgets are usually tight and time or helpers are not limitless, it takes great determination to establish a clear set of priorities in your programme, distinguishing between the essential and the marginal. Don't raise expectations which you can't possibly hope to satisfy. The temptation is to try to do everything at once and so you end up by spreading your effort and cash too thinly for real effect. By carefully evaluating your programme at key points, you are better able to rearrange the priorities. Always think ahead to the next move, the next opportunity to be grasped or problem solved. But don't be discouraged if at first you don't succeed in achieving your objectives. Analyse what went wrong and try again.

Never be afraid of seeking help from other people in the PR

world. There may well come a time when you need additional or specialist outside help. This could mean commissioning a PR consultant or agency on an *ad hoc* or continuous basis. It will depend on your exact needs and, of course, your financial resources. Before you commit yourself, choose your consultant with care, making sure he or she is experienced, right for your organisation and can work both imaginatively and practically with you and your colleagues. It helps to study consistent local PR success stories and find out exactly who initiated and carried them out. But, as a more formal line of advice the Public Relations Consultants Association, to which over 100 of the leading UK consultancies belong, publishes an excellent booklet *Selecting and Employing a Public Relations Consultancy* from which the following extract is a useful sample of the guidance given:

> When selecting a PR consultancy the usual practice is to create a shortlist, and to do this one needs to find those consultancies which satisfy certain criteria. You thus need to ask a number of questions about each consultancy:
>
> Does it have experience in the fields you are concerned with, or would a completely fresh approach be more appropriate (bear in mind that PRCA consultancies are forbidden to handle conflicting accounts without the consent of those concerned)?
>   What is its professional background and what examples can it provide of relevant competent PR activity?
>   What is the firm's reputation?
>   Who are its present clients, what is the rate of client turnover, how long has it been serving current clients?
>   Does the consultancy have the facilities and expertise you require (you may need a home economist, a computer expert, a chemical engineer, etc.)?

There are many ways, too, in which you can develop your own capability and interest in the scope and detail of public relations through reading further and taking a close interest in how other organisations behave publicly, including your competitors. Membership of the Institute of Public Relations, which seeks to promote a greater awareness of the importance of PR through higher standards and better techniques, is an essential consideration for anyone increasingly involved in practical PR. If you have time you may wish to go on a public relations course of which there are several excellent examples ranging from a one-day introductory course to the authoritative, intensive residential five-day course, *Public Relations—principles and practice*, run by CAM Foundation Limited, an organisation which is primarily devoted to training for higher standards in PR and advertising.

A final word of advice. Good public relations is down-to-earth and practical. Vague generalisations or expressions of good intentions seldom create credibility. Being practical depends on the specific and detailed. For a small organisation to wish vaguely to be seen as a good neighbour is not enough. That wish must be translated into specific initiatives, establishing direct lines of personal communication with key local opinion formers ('know and be known'!), showing how the company brings distinct benefits to the locality either by orders won or supplies purchased from local businesses or how a sound, efficient and useful voluntary organisation can earn the enthusiasm, respect and gratitude of a whole community.

So in outlining the general principles and describing some of the basic techniques and potential of good PR, it all comes back to asking five simple but very fundamental questions:

WHAT are we trying to achieve?
WHO are we aiming at?
WHAT do we want to say?
HOW do we get it across?
DID it work?

Getting good publicity is the privilege and responsibility of communicating ideas and reliable information, arousing interest, stimulating constructive action which involves and helps other people, and so creates credibility. Above all PR can build and maintain a pattern of good working relationships which inspire trust and goodwill as well as achieve objectives.

Appendix 1:
Case Studies of PR in Action

This section complements previous basic principles by illustrating ways in which public relations practice has helped a selection of small companies and voluntary organisations—and what has been learnt as a result.

The Camden Garden Centre

The Camden Garden Centre at 66 Kentish Town Road, London NW1, started business in March 1983 on a previously derelict site owned by the local council. It is the creation of an imaginative and socially aware entrepreneur, Gurmukh Singh, born in Singapore, who has been successfully concerned with starting a number of businesses which create jobs, particularly for young people. Backed by the council and Wellcome Trust, the centre is run on a self-financing basis by a charitable trust which provided jobs for seven unemployed young people and offered a superb management opportunity to two young managers, Richard Jackson and Adam Caplin, already experienced in gardening and nursery work.

The important point is that this is not another trendy place for the affluent middle-class locals to buy plants and gardening paraphernalia. It does offer such a service with a superb product range, certainly, but, more important, it is a multi-racial community project aiming to employ and train unemployed young people, and to keep them employed. But this difference proved initially to be a considerable PR challenge to Richard Jackson. He took advice from his five man trust and also from a PR consultant. An attractive leaflet for the opening was designed by design consultant Wolff Olins 'in return for gardening services'.

Other than for the opening, a detailed PR programme was not prepared for the centre. Feeling that he had a good story to tell, Richard Jackson decided on a dual opening, one for the press and one for the public. TV naturalist David Bellamy was booked but had to cancel at the last minute. Fortunately, Hannah Gordon, herself a keen gardener, agreed to fill the gap. The press had been mailed invitations a month previously but Richard Jackson was dismayed to find that many had been mislaid in the post or ignored. So, although a number of journalists turned up for the opening, they were not the ones who really counted. A leading lady gossip-column writer came and all she managed to produce was a snide paragraph about 'another trendy garden centre'. There was more luck with television, doing before and after features. However, both Capital Radio and LBC took a real interest in the project and as a result many different initiatives have followed, including gardening advice for children, 'phone-ins, chat shows and regular talks on gardening topics.

Although the PR build-up was rather slower than at first envisaged, the Camden Garden Centre's success was marked by the doubling of sales budget in the first year. What are the main PR lessons learnt by Richard Jackson for this type of venture? However 'newsy' you may think you are, make sure you identify the key journalists who matter to you and try to forge a good rapport with them by inviting them individually to give them 'exclusive' treatment. It is also necessary to persevere with certain journalists. For example, the trade press, because their invitations were not followed up with a 'phone call, ignored the opening completely, dismissing it, again, as another trendy garden centre, though later came to recognise its interest and feature its work. A strong and unusual human-interest story took some time to grab people's attention.

Fast Engineering Limited

One of the basic marketing truths which Ulsterman Seamus Connolly has been able to demonstrate in successfully developing his County Antrim-based company, Fast Engineering Limited, is that as well as a good idea for a product, you need good business planning and market research. Mr Connolly, a former lecturer at Ulster Polytechnic had six years' preparation before he was able to find a product which started off as an idea for a child's swimming pool and materialised into a prize-winning invention for the manufacture of a new type of portable 2,000 gallon storage tank. Unpacked from a 5ft × 17in × 17in box weighing about 150lb the Fastank comprising a lightweight aluminium frame and durable PVC covered fabric is capable of erection in ten minutes by unskilled labour. About eighty per cent of the tanks sold in the company's first full year of operations have been shipped abroad. Seamus Connolly sought a market share of less than 0.0065 per cent. Infinitesimal though that may seem it will bring Fast Engineering a £5 million turnover by the fifth year. Connolly is concentrating on the Third World's need for simple, quickly erected water-storage and treatment tanks. This careful planning has given him an immense publicity boost on three occasions to date.

In 1982 Seamus Connolly reached the finals of the Bank of Ireland 'Start Your Own Business' competition and won a £10,000 award in the British Technology Group's Academic Enterprise Competition later the same year. He had confidence in his idea and saw the publicity value of the type of competition which evaluates both the financial and design consideration. The benefits to a small business of coming under the wing of a major competition sponsoring organisation were again proved by his winning Mobil's £10,000 first prize in their 1983 Design Award for small firms. 276 entries for this award were whittled down to a final 40 who were invited to exhibit at the Design Centre in London. As well as the cash, marketing and promotional advice were available from Mobil. Connolly spent the £10,000 to create two extra jobs in his firm which now employs ten with a target of thirty by the third year's full operation.

While he professes not to have had a specific publicity programme on paper, saying that it all 'came with success', he put in a lot of work himself in sending out press releases, and in reacting very quickly to letters and enquiries resulting from extensive coverage on local radio and TV. Particularly important to his company and its export potential in the Third World have been the COI and the BBC World Service.

Winning such prestigious prizes so early in his company's development has been an immense boost to morale and business but the resulting publicity must be regarded with realism and care. Too much publicity with its snowball effect can be time consuming and costly in terms of personal effort which detracts from the main business interest and the need to cope with demand. Customers' goodwill can be endangered if deliveries suffer. But with his business acumen and skill as an engineer, Seamus Connolly knows how to use PR intelligently, and if he can be helped towards his targets by courtesy of big organisations he is all the happier.

'One of Gillie's'

'One of Gillie's', based at Llantrithyd in South Glamorgan, was established in 1980 in mail-order beachwear, especially bikinis, by Gillie Williams and a friend in partnership. The special feature of this business is that the tops and bottoms are sold in separate sizes. It also offers an exceptionally large-size range of garments which are made in all-cotton fabrics. The original idea began when Gillie Williams used to have to make clothes for her small children because she couldn't find what she wanted in the shops. One-off designs in evening wear and beachwear followed. But she realised that there was a real problem with beachwear. Women bought a bikini from a shop, the top fitted and the bottom didn't or vice-versa. Urged on by a friend, she decided to start a mail-order business which allowed customers to order the size they really wanted. Today, with her HQ in her own home, she has four regular workers plus a back-up team of part-timers if demand surges.

One of Gillie's is a considerable commercial success because, as a bright and original idea, it has filled market needs. Gillie Williams planned her own publicity programme, choosing a combination of small-space advertising in the fashion pages of national newspapers and women's magazines and of letters to the editorial staff of similar publications. An agency did the advertising but Gillie handled the PR herself. A simple but very attractive brochure was designed, with drawings by her daughter, which is mailed together with an easy-to-follow pattern card of fabrics. New designs of garment are added from time to time, although the range remains simple. Confident that she has a proven idea, her PR approach is basic: 'Keep writing to fashion editors. Find something newsworthy in the business for them to hang an idea on'.

Editorial coverage in the fashion pages has built up in a most encouraging way. In 1983, for example, One of Gillie's was featured in the *Guardian*, *Observer*, *Woman's Realm*, *Family Circle*, *Patterns*, *Weight Watchers*, *Into Shape* and *What Diet*. The piece about her in the *Guardian* led to an interview on BBC TV Wales News Magazine, all of which has resulted in shoals of correspondence and resulting business for the bikinis.

The analysis of business in 1983: 40 per cent of orders resulted from her PR effort and the free editorial mentions, 35 per cent from paid advertising and 25 per cent in repeat business from previous customers.

Survival Aids Limited

Survival Aids Limited, based in the small Cumbrian village of Morland near Penrith, manufactures and supplies personal survival equipment for military and serious outdoor leisure use. Over 200 such survival aids are marketed in the UK and overseas via mail order and a network of retail stockists. The brain child of ex-army Captain Nick Steven, who established it in 1979, the business today employs twenty-seven people and has a turnover of over £¾ million. Although Survival Aids with a unique product range had a relatively unexploited market, Nick Steven has been able to put to the best possible effect his army awareness of the value of good PR in the development of the business. A measure of success must be the fact that British soldiers actually buy the company's products out of their own pockets.

Publicity was planned to create widespread awareness of the company's capabilities in the UK and overseas. Although the Survival Aids board is brimful of ideas themselves, they retain an ex-journalist self-employed PR consultant. The publicity initiatives, which are many and varied, have followed a press launch for the company, including national and local TV and radio coverage and a regular pattern of press releases. But it is clear that Survival Aids has gone out of its way as a company to ensure that people are made aware of its intrinsic interest and value. The company appears to be keenly people-oriented. The telephonist has a bright, friendly, helpful manner. Order forms are presented with a special message from marketing director, Freddy Markham. The catalogue is a colourful mine of valuable information. There is a newsletter and a variety of wallcharts illustrating survival techniques. Special authoritative articles appear in the appropriate publications under the name of a director of the company. Displays at conferences are held as well as open days so that members of the local community can find out more about the company. Lectures are given to special interest groups. But one of the most convincing initiatives has been the holding of special survival courses which, for a fee, convince participants of the worth of the product. PR is a proven business aid for Nick Steven and his colleagues. He reckons that the business received £1,000 per month of 'free advertising' via articles, new product reviews and general press exposure.

Survival Aids has a healthy respect for the press but has learnt not to expect too much from journalists who may ignore press releases, fail to turn up at press conferences or create totally unexpected angles to stories. Nick Steven counsels sensible caution with all press enquiries. 'Ensure mind is engaged before opening mouth; think who the news might offend/alert/interest', he advises.

Recently Survival Aids had an extra publicity boost when the village of Morland won a £1,000 rural employment award in 1983 in a contest sponsored by the Council for Small Industries in Rural Areas (COSIRA) and the Country Landowners Association. The competition is aimed at creating more jobs in the countryside by encouraging the establishment of small businesses in converted buildings. In the case of Morland, virtually a complete village has been transformed. Survival Aids occupying the former mill and village school has become in a number of ways the focal point of this village.

W. R. Outhwaite and Son

W. R. Outhwaite and Son, ropemakers in the Yorkshire Dales market town of Hawes, dates from 1841 when it catered for local farmers' needs. In 1973 it was bought by Peter Annison, a textiles lecturer at Trent Polytechnic, anxious to escape the academic rat race, with his wife Ruth. The Annisons have breathed new life into this business, investing in new building and machinery, to the point where fifteen people are employed and the rope-works is a focal point of tourist visitors in the town, catering for much wider markets than ever before. As well as a busy retail outlet, they have a thriving mail order business in church bell ropes, domestic and ornamental barrier and bannister ropes, macrame cords and equestrian products. The business is well integrated into the local community, despite the fact that the Annisons are 'in-comers', because shrewd Yorkshire folk have been impressed by their hard work and professionalism.

Helped not inconsiderably by Ruth Annison's interests as a freelance journalist, a publicity programme was devised with two simple objectives: first, to increase visitor trade ('If people were coming to watch us work, they might as well be persuaded to buy things from us'), and second to promote new products. The specific initiatives used have included small advertisements in selected publications, for example local tourist guides and the *Dalesman* magazine, simple, bold leaflets and participation in several exhibitions, such as the Great Yorkshire

Show, and a lapel badge 'I've met the Hawes ropemaker'.

The Annisons admit that it is only recently that they have come to realise the cost-effectiveness of editorial PR as compared with paid advertisements. They have certainly built up their visitors through appearances on television and interviews on radio, but have found that promotion of their newer manufactured products has been more difficult. They regard PR as a long-term process requiring constant effort, with results often coming from unexpected quarters. But when PR works it stimulates business in a most encouraging way. As an example, the Annisons cite their range of wooden 'pulls' for bathroom lights or roller blinds. Samples were sent to six magazines. Only *Homes and Gardens* responded with a short editorial in the May 1983 issue. At the end of July orders were still flowing in and three other publications have since been in touch.

Peter and Ruth Annison have been prepared to experiment and learn from their efforts. It is important for them to have good colour as well as black and white photographs available to make it easy for a magazine to illustrate a feature. They code addresses to measure response. They make a point now of systematically contacting editorial staffs of publications via press releases on new developments or any other newsworthy event concerning the business. One such event, a special computer course for beginners organised for Outhwaite staff and others, was such a success that a repeat was held for a wider group. Never forget though that a number of the smaller publications depend for their life blood on smaller companies like W. R. Outhwaite buying advertising space. W. R. Outhwaite & Son is a good example of an old business revitalised and one increasingly conscious of the value of publicity to gain extra business. The latest initiative is a small paperback about the company and its history.

Save Stawley School Action Committee

Stawley Parish is a scattered community, comprising five small villages near Wellington in Somerset. It has a village primary school with approximately 28 children and 2 teachers. Back in 1979 plans were announced by the local education authority for closing the school because of falling rolls and rising costs. But the LEA did not reckon on the strength of local feeling in Stawley and the ability of a group of people who, as pressure to close the school mounted, formed themselves into a committee in 1979, the Friends of Stawley School (registered as a PTA with charitable status), to channel their feeling into purposeful and successful action. In April 1983 Secretary of State for Education, Sir Keith Joseph, ordered that the school should remain open.

Success came only after a major setback and much hard work in dealing with officialdom and organising local support and funds. The bulk of this work fell to a six-man sub-committee, the Save Stawley

School Action Committee, under the Chairmanship of Mrs Peggy Wotton, the local postmistress. A further 50 local people were actively involved in the campaign at one time or another.

In 1981 the committee's representations led to the LEA's Statutory Notice to close the School being declared invalid because of a technicality over its publication. Disappointment soon followed because in September 1982 the LEA published fresh closure notices and so the whole procedure began all over again.

Through 1982 and into 1983 the Save Stawley School Action Commitee prepared a detailed case for retaining the school and mobilised further local support. By involving Taunton's MP, the Rt Hon Edward du Cann, a meeting was arranged in December 1982 with Dr Rhodes Boyson, the Education Under-Secretary so that a closely reasoned 11 page memorandum, supported by maps and many photographs, could be presented to him by a small deputation. One of their stronger claims was that the Somerset County Council had misread the situation and had underestimated the numbers of children likely to use the school in the mid-eighties and beyond, as well as understating the increased costs and personal problems of younger children travelling up to 11 miles each way to alternative schools. In March the good news came that Stawley School was saved and so the committee was disbanded.

Right from the beginning, the committee decided to use the press, local radio and TV as much as possible and, recognising that there was already an underlying sympathy towards the retention of rural schools, appointed one of their members as press officer. The fundamental aim was to use the press to inform those in the area of this committee's action and progress as well as canvassing specific support. It was a solid, well-executed communication exercise and so caught the media's imagination because it was informative rather than 'pushy'. Towards the end, the media were asking the committee for stories.

Certainly the media kept everyone in touch but at the core of the campaign was good management and drive leading firmly into the corridors of power in Whitehall. At each crucial stage the press were well briefed. Mrs Wotton, as chairman, and their press officer were always ready with 'quotes' which crisply summarised the situation or made a constructive comment. When Sir Keith Joseph announced his decision to keep the school open, Mrs Wotton remembered to thank the press for their help amongst the other supporting organisations.

The Link Club

The Guiseley Link Gateway Club in West Yorkshire was established in 1969 as a voluntary group, with no paid staff, not only to provide leisure pursuits for mentally handicapped people with ages from sixteen to middle age, but to create a link between handicapped and non-handicapped and between the parents of handicapped people. The latter 'links' have proved to be a significant factor in the club's success. Today the club caters for seventy mentally handicapped people. Activities include pottery, metalwork, cookery, art and craft work, drama, dancing and a wide range of sporting activities. It meets once a week but also organises special weekend and holiday events. Four years after its start, the Link Club took on four further-education tutors and a club leader who was trained as a youth leader, now being paid by the Leeds Education Authority. As well as the local authority's close support, during the life of this club to date approximately one hundred non-handicapped young people, aged from sixteen to twenty have been involved as volunteers, some for only a few weeks, others for up to five years. The use of volunteers remains a vital component of the club's philosophy in working to create a link between the handicapped and non-handicapped.

Publicity for this club has been developed mainly with the aim of recruiting volunteers, raising funds for the club's activities and transport needs, informing parents in the area and increasing awareness of mental handicap. The local media have been used frequently when any particularly newsworthy event occurs. On each occasion, opportunity is taken in a suitable 'quote' from a club official to outline its aims and activities. There is also involvement in local galas. Floats are created for gala processions and a publicity booth is set up to give further information. One particularly successful publicity initiation was the involvement of four students from Trinity and All Saints College, Leeds, on a media course. This was a project for their final year and formed part of their degree assessment. The students published posters and leaflets about the club and also spoke on local radio. Directly attributable to their efforts was the recruitment of twelve volunteers.

The Link Club has not sought professional PR advice. In looking back over their PR efforts over the years, the club's organisers have learnt several valuable lessons. In using an interesting club event as a focus for publicity, it is important to keep the news release brief, punchy and, most important, not to branch out too much into more philosophical aspects of this club's activities. They have found it wise to avoid confusion with the usual public image of mental handicap; that the mentally handicapped are 'eternal' children, passive recipients of kindness, needing sympathy. The club has also learnt not to over-expose itself in publicity, but to reserve contact with the media for the important and really newsworthy event.

Plain English Campaign

The 'Plain English Campaign' was founded and launched in 1979 by two individualists with a real mission in life. From their present base in Manchester, Chrissie Maher and Martin Cutts decided to declare war on all gobbledegook and jargon in official forms, whether issued by national or local government, large companies or any other organisation which tortures the English language to the frustration and confusion of ordinary people. Britain has more official forms in circulation from Whitehall than any other western nation at an estimated total annual cost of £200 million. It has also been estimated that cutting the errors made in form-filling by only 1 per cent could save up to £1 million a year, as well as relieving much personal worry and distress.

Encouraged by an interest which Liverpool City Council and also the Department of Health and Social Security had already shown in their work, Chrissie Maher and Martin Cutts started their Plain English Campaign by shredding up hundreds of official forms and leaflets outside the Houses of Parliament in July 1979. This achieved their objective of forcing government and other official organisations to take notice of public discontent by capturing the fancy of the media, which the two were quick to exploit by an aggressive follow-up campaign. Later the same year Chrissie Maher turned up at 10 Downing Street, dressed as a gorilla, the 'Gobbledegook Monster' to deliver a copy of their new magazine *Plain English*.

Since then the Plain English Campaign with an enthusiastic backing from the National Consumer Council, has gathered momentum and influence, chiefly by seeking to give advice and help to organisations on how forms can be improved. In 1980 the first Plain English Awards Competition was introduced with six winners and a hundred booby prizes, the latter being a waste-paper bin sent to organisations who created unreadable, incomprehensible bumf. Booby prizes in later years have included 2lb of tripe. Even the government as the prime culprit heeded their message by introducing a programme in 1981, under the aegis of Lord Rayner, then Mrs Thatcher's adviser on Whitehall efficiency, to simplify official language and reduce the number of forms in use.

Today the campaign, with the help of a number of volunteers, continues its work in persuading government departments to use plain English and clear design in forms, leaflets, letters and agreements, as well as vetting new forms and researching issues from the consumer viewpoint, for example the gobbledegook in hire-purchase and insurance policies. Training courses are given on plain English and form design. Publications now include the *Plain English Training Kit* and *Writing Plain English* as well as the quarterly magazine *Plain English*.

Chrissie Maher and Martin Cutts, as experienced journalists themselves, have a shrewd eye for what makes 'news'. Probably every local, national and appropriate trade paper has covered the campaign at least twice, as have most local radio stations; 50 per cent of UK's TV stations have featured the duo. But what is obvious from the Plain English Campaign is the effect that a carefully planned, imaginative programme of positive and lively ideas can have on organisations, the media and the general public. Instead of stereotyped protest the campaign offers practical help and goes out of its way to stimulate initiatives. 'Keep coming up with a new angle' is their motto—and it seems to work admirably.

Bliss

Bliss (Baby Life Support Systems) is a charity founded in 1979 to raise money to buy equipment, ranging from incubators to monitors and respirators for donation to special-care/intensive-care baby units in hospitals and to sponsor the training of doctors and nurses in the care of sick new-born babies. The underlying aim is to ensure that all hospitals in Britain have the equipment they need to look after new-born babies who are sick at birth and to prevent death or handicap.

With up to 10,000 babies at risk each year and a critical shortage of NHS facilities, the task set by BLISS of trying to help 3,000 of these seems formidable. When founders Susanna Cheal and Joan Bertorelli originally called together twenty interested people, they managed to collect only £10.31 between them. Yet since registration as a charity in 1980, BLISS has raised over £⅓ million and donated equipment to more than fifty hospitals. It has also instituted the BLISS Training Fellowship for a senior registrar to train in neonatal paediatrics. With a nationwide membership of over 1,000 BLISS has an executive council of fifteen and a fund-raising committee which gives help, if needed, to the many fund-raising groups around the country.

The important point about BLISS is that everyone works voluntarily. There are no paid full-time officials. BLISS has been able, however, to enlist a number of 'star' patrons, including Joan Collins, who became interested in BLISS's work after visiting the hospital which cared for her daughter who was badly injured in a road accident, Michael Aspel, father of a premature baby, and Jonathan Aitken MP whose premature twins were saved by intensive care. BLISS has also a prestigious medical advisory committee which allocates equipment in the wisest way.

BLISS's publicity programme has three aims: first, to stimulate new membership and increase fund-raising potential; second, to stimulate direct donations; and third, to ensure that BLISS is regarded as a responsible and effective charity in the minds of the medical profession and general public. PR activity centres on the national press, TV and radio, women's magazines and local media, the last tying in with the local fund-raising ventures. As BLISS is donating equipment to hospitals throughout the year, this provides a constant programme of small PR initiatives, such as 'handing over' ceremonies. A major story (for example a large donation) is linked to a 'personality'. Hence, actress Joan Collins handed over BLISS equipment to the hospital which helped her daughter after her accident. She became a vice-president and raised £13,000 from a TV appeal. When it was clear that the Short Report on Perinatal and Neonatal Mortality was not going to be adopted by the government in 1980, BLISS arranged to deliver a letter stating its case to Mrs Thatcher. Before invited newsmen, the letter was transported along Downing Street in an incubator. As well as regular contact with the women's and medical press two important seminars have been held on neonatal care which have been well covered.

By recognising these at an early stage, BLISS has made the most of the considerable talents of its voluntary helpers; for example, the press officer used to be a PR consultant. As a result of well-managed team work BLISS has been very successful in gaining new members and donations plus sales of such items as birth-announcement cards. But well-planned media coverage has accounted for 75 per cent of BLISS's membership and therefore 25 per cent of its income.

Simple PR lessons learnt include checking that an 'event' date does not clash with any other, that a call is made to the news desk a day or so before any press event to make sure that the invitation or information has not been forgotten or mislaid, and, finally, that too much is not expected from the press, especially as far as the nationals are concerned—such is the savage competition for space.

Elemore Community Association

The Elemore Community Association at Hetton-le-Hole, Tyne and Wear, was originally a typical north-east village colliery welfare organisation. In 1974 the colliery closed and it was taken over by the local authority, later becoming a community association. Recognising the acute need for modern facilities in the area for sporting and youth activities, a working party, consisting of representatives of Sunderland Social Services, local councillors and youth leaders, produced a plan to develop a multi-purpose sports hall. Their proposals were announced in 1979 for a £60,000 scheme consisting of a leisure complex for different age groups including workshop facilities and open space for outdoor activities. The working party, after being given the go-ahead to apply for grants from the Department of Education and Sunderland Education Council, which would total £45,000 if successful, launched an appeal to raise money for the balance of £15,000.

Then began an intensive campaign to raise the money by various activities in the area, spurred on by a very tight schedule for building the hall on earmarked land. Encouraged by the knowledge that national government would provide approximately 50 per cent and local government 25 per cent of the cost, the working party was confident that its share could easily be raised. Then the government's cut-backs in public spending caused a severe set-back to their plans. Instead of £15,000, the total to be raised by voluntary effort rose to £23,000. Another blow was the unexpected opposition by residents of an old people's home who started a petition to prevent work beginning on the new complex next door to them, fearing noise and disruption to their lives, even though a number of them had attended the various public meetings when plans and progress were fully aired. Personal contact by the working-party chairman succeeded in dispelling misconceptions.

As well as public meetings, the widespread distribution of leaflets and regular editorial coverage in the local press, the working party staged an exhibition of the architect's plans and sketches. The fund raising gathered pace with a variety of events including sponsored slimming, junior discos, summer fairs and concerts, and a cricket match between Hetton and Radio Newcastle. But the major success was a 'swim-along' with Olympic star David Wilkie which raised £4,000 and autographed certificates were given to the children who took part.

A very close link was forged between the working party and local reporters which meant that every news point and event was always fully covered. The chairman of Elemore Community Association, Jim Heslop, was ever willing to be interviewed, using wise 'quotes' to steer a way through the intricacies of local politics for the benefit of the project. It is as much a testimony to the working party's drive as to the goodwill and support of the local community that £23,000 was raised in two years. The fact that the government's contribution was cut back seemed to make the organisers of the voluntary effort even more determined to succeed.

The Easington Lane Sports Hall was officially opened in September 1981 by the chairman of the local council. Two days later tragically, the project's driving force, Jim Heslop, died of a heart attack.

Yorkshire Dales Society

The Yorkshire Dales Society was established in 1981 'to protect and enhance the Yorkshire Dales heritage' by the author Colin Speakman who now works for the Countryside Commission. As an independent non-profit-making voluntary organisation funded by subscription and donations and supported by grants and voluntary services, it is perhaps complementary to the more narrowly constituted Dales National Park, which is a statutory body with official planning powers and other duties or sanctions. The society seeks 'to bring together those who live and work in the Dales with those who love and visit the Dales, for the good of the Dales'.

With the mounting pressure on the amenities of tourist focal points thanks to the fantastic impact of the James Herriot books and TV programmes, it is important that there should be a body which can stimulate wider and more serious interest amongst the Dales people themselves in the ways in which they live and work, the well-being and balance of the local economy, and the landscape, rather than stimulate this interest in migratory tourists.

The society, which is run by a sixteen-man committee of management, organises a calendar of events for both members and the general public, including day seminars (on Dales transport, for example), open meetings on Dales issues, lectures, visits and guided walks. The society also makes representations on other Dales matters to the local authorities and publishes a quarterly *Review* with original articles and a diary of events within the Dales. There are other occasional leaflets, like *Great Little Museums of the Dales*.

Membership has built up to over 300 since 1981. This was achieved by means of a simple leaflet, widely distributed, incorporating a membership application form, by two advertisements in the *Dalesman* which is read by the society's target audience and by personal contact by Colin Speakman and his committee of management. These efforts have been aided by editorial coverage of events and publications in the Yorkshire and Tees/Tyne press. If there are issues of prime importance to the Dales, these provide an eagerly seized opportunity for a PR 'peg'. For example, the closure announcement by British Rail of the spectacular 72 mile Settle–Carlisle rail link across the Pennines in 1983 gave Colin Speakman, posed against the gaunt beauty of the Ribblehead Viaduct, the chance to voice the society's fervent opposition in the *Sunday Times*.

Colin Speakman finds that membership growth is sporadic, usually following from PR coverage or a special event, but he admits that it is sometimes hard to overcome people's resistance to joining the society. It relies on local loyalties and broad interests in a particular area rather than high-profiled matters of more urgent concern. PR advice is readily available from the Countryside Commission but the society is now seeking specific aid from a PR/fund-raising consultant who will perhaps be able to sharpen staunch Yorkshire pride into a fresh set of initiatives to attract wider attention and funds.

The Castle Hotel, Taunton, Somerset

'Once part of the old Norman fortress, the Castle has been welcoming travellers to Taunton since the 12th century...' is the opening sentence of the Castle Hotel's brochure. But the family-owned hotel is a very up-to-date and lively operation today, employing fifty peole, promoting its many attractions to a widening number of different markets. Its managing director is Christopher Chapman, a former advertising man and the fourth generation of his family in hotels. He joined his father in 1976 as, significantly, marketing manager, before becoming MD in 1981. He took a close look at how the hotel could be developed and promoted as a product rather than just a charming local amenity.

Faced with empty rooms at weekends he identified three new markets for the hotel: the UK business market (conferences as well as a pleasant base for area business visits), the UK leisure market (short breaks and special interest weekends) and the overseas market (North America in particular).

A typical innovation is a delightful weekend experience called 'A Taste of Honey, Cheese and Cider' assembled by Christopher Chapman and his head chef. This, in addition to sumptuous dinner menus, offers visits to Lord Chewton's farm at Chewton Mendip to see cheese and butter being made, the makers of Sheppy's Farmhouse Cider at Bradford-on-Tone, a family enterprise started in the eighteenth century, and 'England's largest honey farm' at South Molton.

In 1981, after the UK hotel industry had experienced a 45 per cent downturn in North American visitors the previous year, Christopher Chapman, another young hotelier and the owner of a sight-seeing service who met up at a conference, decided to attack the market head-on with what was unashamedly a publicity 'stunt'. Billed as 'Three British Gentlemen' and kitted out by the appropriate St James's shops with bowlers, shirting and umbrellas, they flew to the US by Concorde before touring Texas, Georgia and the Midwest by Rolls-Royce. They spoke at conventions, on radio and TV shows, and called on a host of travel agencies. It worked splendidly and resulted in increased business at their hotels.

Christopher Chapman puts great stress on top-quality brochures and other print-work and also feels that it is vital to set clear PR objectives. He makes a special point of knowing who really counts in his branch of the media—the travel writers (there are eighty of them in the UK alone). He then prefers to work with them on a one-to-one basis rather than scattering his PR seed too widely, by identifying a particular publication, picking plenty of lead time, and then 'courting' the appropriate travel writer until the idea for a feature on the Castle Hotel is 'sold' as an exclusive. He also tries to anticipate the special areas of interest about which the press may wish to write. He mails all travel editors at a time when they are planning, say, Christmas or Easter features. Working closely with tourist boards is another important element in this PR mix.

Today the Castle Hotel, thanks to this strong sense of marketing publicity, has benefited from a dramatic growth in bookings in the three target markets, particularly with UK leisure and overseas guests, now accounting for 20 per cent and 28 per cent respectively of total bookings.

Appendix 2: Checklists

A Basic Publicity Checklist

1 Do you know your own organisation, what makes it different, special?
2 Do you have a written set of objectives and a plan of action?
3 Are you clear how you would like to be seen as an organisation, the image you would like to have?
4 How does your image match up with the reality? Is there a credibility gap? How do you find out?
5 Do you have an overall public relations policy? Is it active or defensive? Do you have a budget for achieving this?
6 Is this policy understood and believed in by your colleagues in the organisation? Do they contribute ideas and play sufficient part in your organisation's PR programme?
7 Are your premises easy to find by a visitor and well maintained?
8 Do you have a clear, consistent and well-designed 'house style'?
9 Are your telephone and reception staff well informed, efficient?
10 What publics, individuals, local community and special groups are important to you? Is there any order of priority? Do you know the key opinion formers and leaders in your industry or community?
11 How do you maintain communication with external groups at present?
12 Do you know what media are important to you?
13 Who is responsible in your absence for dealing with general PR matters, and the media in particular?
14 Do you have a contingency plan for dealing with bad news, emergencies, accidents, complaints, including a prepared 'response' statement, and back-up questions with suggested answers?
15 Do you have regular sessions with colleagues to check on potential publicity, newsworthy activities and events?
16 Are your internal communications working well? Do you have regular meetings to brief policy, progress and problems?
17 Do you have good up-to-date photographs which illustrate your organisation's activities effectively? Are there up-to-date portrait photographs of key people?
18 Do you have a simple, clear brochure which sets out the aims and activities of your organisation? Do you ensure that new publications are properly distributed to key publics?
19 Do you issue regular newsletters, leaflets, to your key publics?
20 Do you take note of other people's successful PR ideas and see if

they could be adapted for your own organisation? Do you study the publicity of your competitors?

21 Do you regularly monitor your public relations programme and adjust your plans accordingly?

22 What more can you do to improve the public awareness, recognition and acceptance of your organisation? What specific action or initiatives are necessary?

23 Could you take more initiative in seeking opportunities to publicise your organisation, by giving talks, writing articles or inviting people to visit?

24 Do you know the people in the media who would write or talk specially about your type of organisation and activities? Do you make a point of maintaining regular contact with them?

25 Do you know who in your organisation has specially useful contacts which can benefit your PR? Do you make use of these?

26 Could you handle a difficult interview by a newspaper, TV or radio reporter? Do you know your own strengths and weaknesses as a communicator? Is there someone, other than yourself, at (or very near) the top of your organisation who is willing and able to be your PR figure-head? He or she will need to have interest, knowledge, status and communication skills. Could you train them?

27 Do you keep adequate and up-to-date mailing lists of the media and other groups or organisations important to you?

28 Do you study and keep for further reference press clippings?

29 Do you take time to study and evaluate the usefulness to your own organisation of the latest communication trends and techniques? Are you as well informed as you should be on the practice and potential of PR?

30 Could you benefit from expert specialist advice on PR matters? Would attending a short course on PR help? Do you know how to find out about the best requirements for your needs?

Checklist for a press release

1 Is there a really topical news story to tell?

2 If others are involved (customers, local authority officials, sponsor, donor, VIP) have they given their full approval to release the story?

3 What has happened (or is about to happen)?

4 Who was involved (or will be involved)?

5 Where did it or will it happen? When? How? Why?

6 Would background notes provide useful additional information?

7 Would an accompanying photograph help the story?

8 Every detail checked: names, titles, relevant personal details (age, marital status, family, education, interests), facts, dates, technical information, any legal problems, confidentiality, commercial security?

9 Has the final press release (date, who to contact for further information) and any accompanying material been checked?

Checklist for a press conference?

1 Is a press conference really necessary? What will it achieve?
2 Who should organise it?
3 Date OK? No conflicting events? Time and place? Refreshments?
4 Who should be invited from the media? Who else should be involved (colleagues, experts, influential supporters, donors)?
5 Invitation letters and/or 'phone calls? A map to find location?
6 What is the exact programme? Tour of premises or other special event? Exhibits? Visual aids?
7 Prepared for awkward, dificult questions?
8 Hand-outs checked and run off for those attending? Background briefing notes necessary?
9 'Phones available for media? Quiet area for TV/radio interviews?
10 Do colleagues/employees know? Is a rehearsal necessary?
11 Identification badges for all those attending?
12 Acceptances checked? Reminders necessary?

Checklist for a seminar or conference

1 Why hold this event? What is to be achieved? Is there a theme?
2 What form of conference? Residential or non-residential?
3 What size event and who should attend? How invite?
4 When and how long? Midweek or weekend? One day, half day?
5 Where? What are the full facilities? Checked personally?
6 What will it cost? Speaker/s' fees and expenses? Price of admission?
7 Who is responsible for making all arrangements?
8 Chairman and speakers? Does each know what is expected of them?
9 Speeches and other material to be issued in advance or afterwards?
10 Programme? Circulate in advance or on day?
11 Are microphones, recording equipment, visual aids OK?
12 A final briefing before the start?

Checklist for open days

1 Who will organise the event? A committee/or individual co-ordinator?
2 Date OK? Time? How long? What will it cost?
3 Who should be invited? Local VIPs? Media? Advance publicity?
4 What type of programme? A tour? What special activities to be laid on (production sequences, displays)?
5 Security and safety? OK for children, disabled visitors?
6 A printed programme (purpose, tour route, history, description of activities, processes)? Signs? Identification badges?
7 Refreshments, toilet facilities?
8 Parking OK? Need to inform police?
9 Numbers checked? Reminders necessary?
10 Staff, colleagues, employees briefed? Who is responsible for VIPs?
11 Welcome arranged on arrival?

Addresses and Further Reading

The Advertising Association,
Abford House, 15 Wilton Road, London SW1V 1NJ *Telephone: 01-828 2771*

The Association of Business Sponsorship of the Arts,
12 Abbey Churchyard, Bath BA1 1LY *Telephone: 0225 63762*

British Institute of Management,
Cottingham Road, Corby, Northants *Telephone: 05363 4222*

Central Office of Information,
Hercules Road, London SE1 7DU *Telephone: 01-928 2345*

Charities Aid Foundation,
48 Pembury Road, Tonbridge, Kent TN9 2JD *Telephone: 0732 356323*

Charity Commission,
14 Ryder Street, London SW1Y 6AH *Telephone: 01-214 6000*

Communication, Advertising and Marketing Education Foundation (CAM),
Abford House, 15 Wilton Road, London SW1V 1NJ *Telephone: 01-828 7506*

Confederation of British Industry (CBI),
Centre Point, 103 New Oxford Street, London WC1A 1DU *Telephone: 01-379 7400*

Co-operative Development Agency,
20 Albert Embankment, London SE1 7TJ *Telephone: 01-211 4633*

Council for Small Industries in Rural Areas (COSIRA),
141 Castle Street, Salisbury, Wiltshire SP1 3TP *Telephone: 0722 6255*

Design Council,
28 Haymarket, London SW1Y 4SU *Telephone: 01-839 8000*

English Tourist Board,
4 Grosvenor Gardens, London SW1W 0DU *Telephone: 01-730 3400*

European Economic Commission,
UK Information Offices, 20 Kensington Palace Gardens, London W8 4QQ *Telephone: 01-727 8090*

Incorporated Society of British Advertisers Ltd (ISBA),
44 Hartford Street, London W1Y 8AE *Telephone: 01-499 7502*

Industrial Society,
Peter Runge House, 3 Carlton House Terrace, London SW1Y 5DG *Telephone: 01-839 4300*

Institute of Marketing,
Moor Hall, Cookham, Maidenhead, Berks SL6 9QH *Telephone: Bourne End (06285) 24922*

Institute of Public Relations,
Gate House, St John's Square, London EC1M 4DH *Telephone: 01-253 5151*

Manpower Services Commission,
Marketing & Information Branch, Moorfoot, Sheffield S1 4PO *Telephone: 0742 753275*

National Association of Citizens' Advice Bureaux,
110 Drury Lane, London WC2B 5SW *Telephone: 01-836 9231*

National Audio-Visual Aids Centre (and Library),
Paxton Place, Gypsy Road, London SE27 9SR *Telephone: 01-761 0904*

National Consumer Council,
18 Queen Anne's Gate, London SW1H 9AA *Telephone: 01-222 9501*

National Council for Voluntary Organisations,
26 Bedford Square, London WC1B 3HU *Telephone: 01-636 4066*

National Federation of Community Organisations,
10 Bayley Street, London WC1B 3HB *Telephone: 01-636 1295*

National Union of Journalists,
314–20 Gray's Inn Road, London WC1X 8DP *Telephone: 01-278 7916*

Public Relations Consultants Association,
37 Cadogan Street, London SW3 2PR *Telephone: 01-581 3951*

Small Firms Division,
Department of Industry, Ashdown House, 123 Victoria Street, London SW1E 6RB *Telephone: Freephone 2444*

Society of Industrial Artists and Designers,
12 Carlton House Terrace, London SW1Y 5AH *Telephone: 01-930 1911*

Further reading

Getting Through: how to make words work for you Godfrey Howard (David & Charles, 1980). *The Company Speaks: communication in modern British management* Graham Kemp (Longman, 1973) O/P. *Manual of Public Relations* Pat Bowman and Nigel Ellis (Heinemann, 1969). *Be Your Own P.R. Man: a public relations guide for the small business man* Michael Bland (Kogan Page, 1981). *Using the Media: how to deal with the press, television and radio* Denis MacShane (Pluto Press, 1979). *The Practice of Public Relations* W. P. Howard (ed) (Heinemann, 1981). *Communicate: Parkinson's Formula for Business Survival* C. Northgate Parkinson/Nigel Rowe (Prentice/Hall International, 1978).

Index